The Ability to Risk

The Ability to Risk

Reading Skills for Beginning Students of ESL

LESLIE J. NOONE

Colorado State University
Intensive English Program

PRENTICE HALL REGENTS, Englewood Cliffs, New Jersey 07632

Library of Congress Cataloging in Publication Data

NOONE, LESLIE J.
    The ability to risk.

    1. English language—Text-books for foreign
speakers. 2. College readers. I. Title.
PE1128.N64 1986   428.6′4   85-3468
ISBN 0-13-000357-3

Editorial/production supervision
and interior design by Martha Masterson
Cover design by Diane Saxe
Manufacturing buyer: Harry Baisley

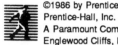

©1986 by Prentice Hall Regents
Prentice-Hall, Inc.
A Paramount Communications Company
Englewood Cliffs, New Jersey 07632

Printed in the United States of America

10

ISBN 0-13-000357-3

Prentice-Hall International (UK) Limited, *London*
Prentice-Hall of Australia Pty. Limited, *Sydney*
Prentice-Hall Canada Inc., *Toronto*
Prentice-Hall Hispanoamericana, S.A., *Mexico*
Prentice-Hall of India Private Limited, *New Delhi*
Prentice-Hall of Japan, Inc., *Tokyo*
Simon & Schuster Asia Pte. Ltd., *Singapore*
Editora Prentice-Hall do Brasil, Ltda., *Rio de Janeiro*

Contents

Preface

The ability to risk is essential in developing efficient reading strategies. Without this skill, students are ineffective in predicting, guessing vocabulary from context, and rapid reading, all of which are skills regularly employed by efficient readers. Since beginning reading students have a tendency to read and decode word by word, they especially need to be encouraged to practice taking risks.

The Ability to Risk is designed for a semester's work (14 weeks) for academically oriented ESL students. This text *teaches* (rather than merely providing practice in using) reading skills that help students take risks.

The text is based on the following assumptions about reading.

1. Reading is not simply a word-by-word decoding process, but rather an active process in which the reader forms hypotheses (based on prior knowledge of the subject and/or familiarity with commonly used rhetorical organizations) and then "tests" these hypotheses against the information contained in the passage.

2. An efficient reader
   recognizes that knowing the meaning of every word is unnecessary in order to understand main ideas.
   is willing to risk (that is, is willing to continue reading with a degree of uncertainty).

possesses the strategies that allow him or her to risk efficiently, such as recognizing the role of examples in a passage and allowing the purpose of the reading to determine which of a number of reading strategies to employ.

3. Rarely does an individual read in order to answer a series of comprehension questions.

To facilitate the students' abilities to risk, the following skills are taught: locating the main idea; scanning; skimming, or previewing; critical thinking; inferencing; information gathering; and guessing vocabulary from context. This text provides reading passages on familiar topics such as the classification of foods and animals, temperatures, family trees, and computers. Since students will be familiar with the content of these passages (from prior knowledge), they will be more willing or able to risk, to be efficient readers. A variety of post-reading activities such as the completion of charts and calendars provide a realistic application of the information read in the passage. Various types of reading, both prose and nonprose, provide students with the opportunity to use the various strategies. In addition, beginning information-gathering skills and study skills such as alphabetizing, using a textbook, and using a dictionary are introduced.

SUGGESTIONS FOR USE

1. In-class reading is extremely important at the beginning of the course so that the teacher can immediately demonstrate that reading word-by-word with a dictionary is neither expected nor desired in this course, or in reading in general. Thus, *The Ability to Risk* is organized so that the early chapters (1–3) contain a large number of nonprose and short prose readings which lend themselves to in-class work.

2. Building beginning students' confidence in their ability to read is essential if they are to continue risking. This text contains numerous exercises of a similar nature. A particular class may not need to complete every exercise. However, the exercises are invaluable for those classes or individuals who require additional practice in that particular skill. For example, students might work in groups or as a class to complete the first calendar-reading exercise. The additional calendar exercises can serve as practice for some or all students (perhaps as homework) and can demonstrate to both students and the teacher that a particular skill has been mastered.

3. As students progress and become more comfortable with risk taking, the reading passages increase in length. These longer readings might be assigned as homework. Assigning an exercise for students to complete after reading is recommended for two reasons. First, this provides a reason for reading, which in turn determines how students are to read. For example, if students are told to read the passage and underline the main idea of each paragraph, they don't need to know every word in the passage. Second, assignments such as this indirectly foster a student's confidence: "I could answer the question(s) without knowing every word."

4. Since beginning students are frequently more willing or able to take short-term risks, they should be encouraged to underline or circle unknown words while they are reading. They can then bring their questions to class, where the teacher and possibly other students can serve as a "dictionary." This procedure builds students' confidence while satisfying their need to "know all the words in English."

5. Each chapter contains exercises of varying difficulty levels so that students' confidence continues to grow. They will find some exercises "easy" while others will prove to be more challenging. They will also find that initially challenging exercises become much easier.

While it is true that almost any text can be modified to "teach" reading strategies, such teaching is possible only when the reader/teacher (1) is aware of the strategies to be taught (many efficient readers are *not* conscious of what they do), and (2) has time to create new or modify existing exercises to accompany a particular text. The goals then of this text are

1. to teach the following reading strategies and skills: how to find the main idea, how to recognize and use examples, how to guess vocabulary from context by using appositives and anaphoric referents, and how to combine information contained in various places in a passage to complete a task.

2. to build the students' confidence so that they are willing to risk while reading.

3. to provide a firm foundation for dealing with the more sophisticated reading passages they will encounter.

4. in short, to RISK.

The teacher's manual includes techniques for teaching, answers to exercises, and suggestions on how to exploit the materials for maximum benefit. Unconsciously efficient readers may find it quite useful.

ACKNOWLEDGMENTS

A most sincere thank you to Mark J. Noone, who created the illustrations for this text. My gratitude to Barbara, Jim, and Polly, who enthusiastically responded to requests for information. A most heartfelt thank you to Eva, Tommy, and especially Brian, who helped me to learn to risk.

Leslie J. Noone
Ft. Collins, CO

The Ability
to Risk

1

The Calendar

ABBREVIATIONS IN DATES

Many times people use abbreviations when they write common words. Abbreviations are short forms of the word. When we write dates, we often use abbreviations for the days of the week and the months of the year.

There are seven days in a week. They are:

Day	Abbreviation
Sunday	Sun.
Monday	Mon.
Tuesday	Tues.
Wednesday	Wed.
Thursday	Thurs.
Friday	Fri.
Saturday	Sat.

There are twelve months in a year. They are:

Month	Abbreviation
January	Jan.
February	Feb.
March	Mar.*
April	Apr.
May	— (no abbreviation)
June	Jun.*
July	Jul.*
August	Aug.
September	Sept.
October	Oct.
November	Nov.
December	Dec.

We also use abbreviations for the numbers in dates. There are two kinds of numbers: cardinal numbers (*one, two, three*) and ordinal numbers (*first, second, third*). Study the numbers and abbreviations that follow.

Cardinal Number		Ordinal Number	Abbreviation
one	1	first	1st
two	2	second	2nd
three	3	third	3rd
four	4	fourth	4th
five	5	fifth	5th
six	6	sixth	6th
seven	7	seventh	7th
eight	8	eighth	8th
nine	9	ninth	9th
ten	10	tenth	10th
eleven	11	eleventh	11th
twelve	12	twelfth	12th
thirteen	13	thirteenth	13th
fourteen	14	fourteenth	14th
fifteen	15	fifteenth	15th
sixteen	16	sixteenth	16th
seventeen	17	seventeenth	17th
eighteen	18	eighteenth	18th
nineteen	19	nineteenth	19th
twenty	20	twentieth	20th
twenty-one	21	twenty-first	21st

*This abbreviation is not always used because the name of the month is short.

twenty-two	22	twenty-second	22nd
twenty-three	23	twenty-third	23rd
twenty-four	24	twenty-fourth	24th
twenty-five	25	twenty-fifth	25th
twenty-six	26	twenty-sixth	26th
twenty-seven	27	twenty-seventh	27th
twenty-eight	28	twenty-eighth	28th
twenty-nine	29	twenty-ninth	29th
thirty	30	thirtieth	30th
thirty-one	31	thirty-first	31st

We use cardinal numbers (*two, three, four*) when the word after the number is plural (ends with *s*). For example:

> There are seven day*s* in a week.
> There are twelve month*s* in a year.
> There are thirty day*s* in June.

We use ordinal numbers (*first, second, third*) after months and after the word *the*. For example:

> I came to the U.S. on *April* 1ˢᵗ.
> I pay for the telephone on *the* third Saturday of every month.

Exercise a

Complete these sentences with the correct word.

1. There are ___seven___ days in a week.
   seventh seven

2. Sunday is the ___first___ day of the week.
   first one

3. Tuesday is the ___third___ day of the week.
   third three

4. Friday is the ___sixth___ day of the week.
   sixth six

5. ___Saturday___ is the seventh day of the week.

6. There are ___twelve___ months in a year.
   twelfth twelve

7. January is the ___first___ month of the year.
   first one

8. There are _____ 24 _____ hours in a day.
   24th   24

9. There are _____ 60 _____ seconds in a minute.
   60th   60

10. There are _____ 52 _____ weeks in a year.
    52nd   52

11. There are _____ 365 _____ days in a year.
    365th   365

12. March is the _____ third _____ month of the year.

13. April is the _____ fourth _____ month of the year.

14. _____ November _____ is the eleventh month of the year.

15. May is the _____ fifth _____ month of the year.

READING CALENDARS

Exercise b

Look at this calendar (figure 1) and answer the questions. Use abbreviations where possible.

1. How many days are there in February? There are _____ 28 _____ days.

2. What is the name of the first day in February? The first day is _____ Sunday _____, Feb. _____ First _____.

3. What is the date of the first Friday in February? It is the _____ sixth _____.

4. How many Sundays are there in February? There are _____ 4 _____ Sundays.

figure 1

February

Sun.	Mon.	Tues.	Wed.	Thurs.	Fri.	Sat.
1	2	3	4	5	6	7
8	9	10	11	12	13	14
15	16	17	18	19	20	21
22	23	24	25	26	27	28

5. What is the date of the second Wednesday in February? The second
   Wednesday is Feb. _eleventh_.

6. What day is Feb. 24th? It is a _tuesday_. It is the fourth
   tuesday in February.

7. Today is Feb. 10th. Yesterday was Feb. _ninth_.
   Tomorrow will be Feb. _eleventh_.

8. A week from Monday, Feb. 16th, is Monday, Feb. 23rd. A week from
   Thursday, Feb. 12th, is _nineteenth_.

9. Today is Monday, Feb. 2nd. A week from today is _Febrary_,
   ninth. A week after the 9th is the _sixteenth_.

10. Today is Wednesday, Feb. 11th. A week ago was Feb.
    Fourth. A week before the 25th was the _eighteenth_.

Exercise c

True or false?

_F_ 1. The first month of the year is February.

_T_ 2. The fifth month of the year is May.

_F_ 3. The last month of the year is November.

_T_ 4. June comes before July.

_T_ 5. May comes after June.

Rewrite the false sentences to make them true.

Exercise d

Look at this calendar (figure 2) and complete the following.

1. There are _4_ Thursdays in November.

2. There are _4_ Mondays in November.

3. Thanksgiving is on the fourth Thursday in November. The date will
   be November _twenty-sixth_.

4. Today is November 7th. It is the _wednesday_ Wednesday in
   November.

(3)

November

Sun.	Mon.	Tues.	Wed.	Thurs.	Fri.	Sat.
				1	2	3
4	5	6	7	8	9	10
11	12	13	14	15	16	17
18	19	20	21	22	23	24
25	26	27	28	29	30	

figure 2

5. Two weeks from today will be November _____ ninth _____.

6. November 30th is the ___ FIFTH ___ Friday in November.

7. Mary will go to the doctor's office on the second Friday in November. She must return two weeks later. When will Mary go to the doctor? Nov. _twenty-thridth_ and Nov. _ninght_ .

8. December 1st is on a ___ Saturday. ___.

Exercise e

Complete this calendar (figure 3).

1. Write the name of this month above the calendar.
2. Write the abbreviations of the days of the week on the calendar.

figure 3

				1ST	2ND	3RD
4th	5th	6th	7th	8th	9th	10th
11th	12th	13th	14th	15th	16th	17th
18th	19th	20th	21ST	22ND	23RD	24th
25th	26th	27th	28th	29th	30th	31ST

(4)

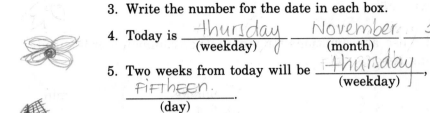

3. Write the number for the date in each box.

4. Today is ___thursday___ ___November___ ___1ˢᵗ___ .
        (weekday)   (month)   (day)

5. Two weeks from today will be ___thursday___ , ___November___
                                 (weekday)   (month)
   ___FiFTheen.___
     (day)

6. There are _____ Mondays in this month.

7. The third Wednesday in this month is the _____ .

Exercise f

Look at this calendar (figure 4) and complete the following.

1. There are ___thirty___ days in May.

2. There are no classes on the third Monday in May. What is the date?
   ___FiFTheenth___ . A week later is the ___twenty second___ .

3. The last day of classes is the second Friday in May. What is the date?
   ___May thirteenth___

4. The final exam is the second Thursday in May. What is the date?
   ___May twelfth___

5. Classes begin again on the fourth Monday in May. What is the date?
   ___May twenty-thirdth___

6. May 15th is the ___third___ Sunday in May.

figure 4

			May			
Sun.	Mon.	Tues.	Wed.	Thurs.	Fri.	Sat.
1	2	3	4	5	6	7
8	9	10	11	12	13	14
15	16	17	18	19	20	21
22	23	24	25	26	27	28
29	30	31				

feet & foot
Ms, Mrs & Miss.

MORE ABBREVIATIONS

We also use abbreviations for many other common words. Study the following list.

1. north	N.	18. minute	min.
2. south	S.	19. foot/feet	ft.
3. east	E.	20. inch	in.
4. west	W.	21. yard	yd.
5. apartment	apt.	22. mile	mi.
6. Street	St. (after a name)	23. kilometer	km.
7. Avenue	Ave. (after a name)	24. kilogram	kg.
8. Drive	Dr. (after a name)	25. pound	lb.
9. Doctor	Dr. (before a name)	26. university	univ.
10. Mister (man)	Mr.	27. Bachelor of Arts	B.A.
11. woman	Ms.	28. Bachelor of Science	B.S.
12. married woman	Mrs.	29. Master of Arts	M.A.
13. unmarried woman	Miss	30. Master of Science	M.S.
14. month	mo.	31. Doctor of Philosophy	Ph.D.
15. year	yr.	32. number	no.
16. week	wk.	33. United States	U.S.
17. hour	hr.	34. dollar	$
		35. et cetera	etc.

Exercise g

What do the italicized abbreviations mean?

1. *Dr.* Smith lives on Shoreline *Dr.*
   Doctor   Drive

2. There are 12 *in.* in one *ft.*
   inch   feet

3. There are 3 *ft.* in one *yd.*
   feet   yard

4. *Mrs.* Black's kitchen is 10 *ft.* by 12 *ft.*
   Mister   feet   foot

5. Do you live on *N.* College *Ave.* or *S.* College *Ave.*?
   North   Avenue   South
   Avenue.

6. Is the store on *E.* Main *St.* or *W.* Main *St.?*

 <u>*East*</u>   <u>*street*</u>   <u>*west*</u>
 <u>*street*</u>

7. A *km.* is shorter than a *mi.*

 <u>*kilometer*</u>   <u>*mile*</u>

8. *Ms.* Brown paid $2.00 for 10 *lbs.* of potatoes.

 <u>*dollar*</u>   <u>*pounds*</u>   <u>*woman*</u>

Exercise h

Read the paragraphs. Circle the abbreviations and tell what they mean.

Education is important to Americans. In the U.S., all children must go to school until they are 16 yrs. old. Most of them continue in school until they graduate from high school. They complete high school at about 18 yrs. of age. Then some people study at a univ. After four years of study there, they graduate with a B.A. or a B.S. degree. Some of them continue to study at the university. They work for graduate, advanced, degrees. These graduate degrees are M.A. or M.S. and Ph.D. degrees.

In Sept., Jamil came to the U.S. to study English. He's living in apt. no. 22 at 1106 S. Florida Dr. He has a small apartment; it is only 15 ft. by 20 ft. He likes it because it's only one mi. from the univ. and it costs just $125 a mo.

Dr. Johnson is an ear specialist. His office is on W. 13th Ave. It is a small office. The waiting room is only 12 ft. 6 in. by 10 ft. Dr. Johnson has two nurses, Mrs. Smith and Ms. Anderson. Mrs. Smith works on Tues., Wed., and Thurs. Ms. Anderson works on Fri. and Sat. The office is closed on Sun. and Mon., so you can't have an appointment on those days. The office is also closed for two wks. in Aug., when Dr. Johnson takes a vacation.

NOTE: In university writing, some of the abbreviations are not common. What are they? Guess.

ALPHABETIZING

One of the most common ways to organize (put together) information is by alphabetizing it. When we alphabetize, we put all the words
beginning with *a* together, all the words beginning with *b* together, etc.

Many things are alphabetized so that we can find the information
we need quickly. For example, dictionaries, telephone books, catalogs
at the library, and indexes at the end of textbooks are all organized
alphabetically. Learning to alphabetize will help you very quickly find
the information you want, such as a word in a dictionary.

Exercise i

Complete the following with the correct letter of the alphabet.

Example: _a_ b c

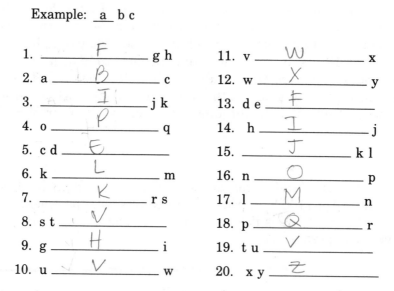

1. _____ F _____ g h   11. v ___ W ___ x
2. a ___ B ___ c   12. w ___ X ___ y
3. ___ I ___ j k   13. d e ___ F ___
4. o ___ P ___ q   14. h ___ I ___ j
5. c d ___ E ___   15. ___ J ___ k l
6. k ___ L ___ m   16. n ___ O ___ p
7. ___ K ___ r s   17. l ___ M ___ n
8. s t ___ V ___   18. p ___ Q ___ r
9. g ___ H ___ i   19. t u ___ V ___
10. u ___ V ___ w   20. x y ___ Z ___

Look at the following group of words.

___ 3 ___ June

___ 2 ___ July

___ 1 ___ January

If we want to alphabetize these words, we look at the first letter of
each word. It is the same, *J*, so we look at the second letters: *Ju, Ju,* and
Ja. The letter *a* is before the letter *u* in the alphabet, so the word
January is the first. Because two words begin with *Ju,* we look at the

third letter: *Ju*n and *Ju*l. The letter *l* is before *n* in the alphabet, so *July* is the second word and *June* is the third.

Exercise j

Alphabetize these groups of words.

I

2 calendar
1 before
3 December
5 September
4 later

II

5 west
2 north
1 east
4 south
3 tenth

III

5 year
4 week
1 day
3 month
2 hour

IV

5 yesterday
2 July
3 Monday
1 April
4 tomorrow

V

2 and
3 are
1 all

VI

3 give
2 gift
1 graduate

VII

1 bad
3 buy
2 boy

VIII

3 drive
2 doctor
1 decide

IX

1 autumn
3 sixth
2 seventh
4 summer

X

3 woman
4 women
1 warm
2 winter

XI

1 right
4 write
3 white
2 wet

XII

1 weather
4 winter
3 windy
2 whole

XIII

3 because
2 bad
1 after
8 snow
9 we
10 year
5 page
7 snake
6 pants
4 black

XIV

8 wild
4 example
10 word
6 only
7 take
9 window
1 ball
2 calendar
3 children
5 old

XV

10 week
3 cat
7 think
8 tiger
1 belt
6 paint
9 walls
2 board
5 October
4 eggs

9

Exercise k

First answer these questions. Then alphabetize your answers to the questions.

1. What are the days of the week? (Use abbreviations.)

MONDAY — Mon
TUESDAY — Tu
WEDNESDAY — WED.
Thrusday — TH
FRIDAY — FRi
SATURDAY — SAT
SUNDAY — SUN

① FRIDAY
② MONDAY
③ SATURDAY
④ SUNDAY
⑤ ThrusDAY
⑥ TUESDAY
⑦ WEDNESDAY

2. What are the months of the year? (Use abbreviations.)

JANUARY —— JAN
February —— Feb
March —— Mar
april —— APR.
MAY —— MAY
June —— JUN
July —— JUL
august —— Aug
september — Sept
October — OCT
November — Nov
December — OEC

3. Name (tell) five parts of the body.

FACE
heart
head
arm
knee.

HW

4. Name three cities in the U.S.

- Washington
- New York
- Illinois

5. Name four animals.

- dog
- cat
- monkey
- elephant

6. Name ten countries.

- Canada
- England
- United States
- Dominican Republic
- Spain
- Germany
- Brazil
- China
- Japan
- France

⑪

2

The Doctor

BODY PARTS

Exercise a

Alphabetize these groups of words.

<table>
<tr><th colspan="2">I</th><th colspan="2">II</th></tr>
<tr><td>2</td><td>foot</td><td>2</td><td>chest</td></tr>
<tr><td>1</td><td>ankle</td><td>5</td><td>shoulder</td></tr>
<tr><td>4</td><td>leg</td><td>4</td><td>neck</td></tr>
<tr><td>5</td><td>toe</td><td>1</td><td>arm</td></tr>
<tr><td>3</td><td>knee</td><td>3</td><td>elbow</td></tr>
<tr><th colspan="2">III</th><th colspan="2">IV</th></tr>
<tr><td>3</td><td>thumb</td><td>4</td><td>hair</td></tr>
<tr><td>1</td><td>finger</td><td>3</td><td>ear</td></tr>
<tr><td>4</td><td>wrist</td><td>1</td><td>cheek</td></tr>
<tr><td>2</td><td>hand</td><td>2</td><td>chin</td></tr>
</table>

12

V

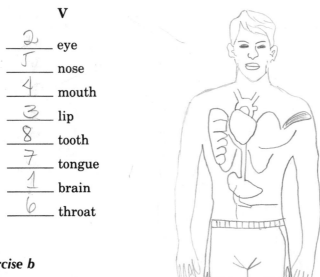

_2___ eye

_5___ nose

_4___ mouth

_3___ lip

_8___ tooth

_7___ tongue

_1___ brain

_6___ throat

Exercise b

Write the correct number on the lines in figures 5 and 6

1. hair	11. leg	21. head
2. face	12. knee	22. ear
3. neck	13. foot (feet)	23. cheek
4. shoulder	14. toe	24. throat
5. arm	15. ankle	25. chin
6. elbow	16. chest	26. lip
7. wrist	17. stomach	27. tongue
8. hand	18. heart	28. tooth (teeth)
9. thumb	19. lung	29. mouth
10. finger	20. brain	30. nose
		31. eye

ANALOGIES

One way of practicing vocabulary is by using analogies. Look at this analogy:

black : white : : big : ___small.___

Look at the first two words, *black* and *white*. *Black* is the opposite of *white*. To complete this analogy, you need to write the word that is the opposite of *big*.

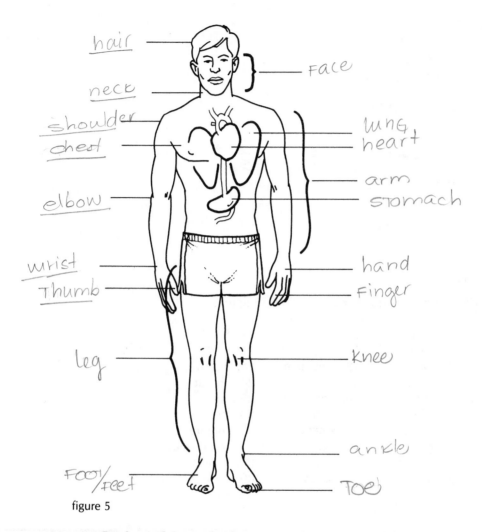

hair

neck

shoulder

chest

elbow

wrist

Thumb

leg

FOOT/Feet

Face

lung
heart

arm
stomach

hand
Finger

knee

ankle

Toe

figure 5

Look at this analogy:

fruit : banana :: car : ___MERCEDES BENZ___.

Banana is one kind of fruit. Write in one kind of car.

Exercise c

Complete the following analogies about parts of the body.

1. ankle : foot :: wrist : ___FINGER.___

14

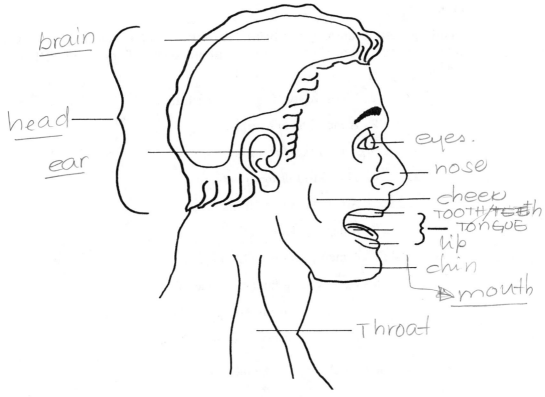

brain

head

ear

eyes.

nose

cheek

TOOTH/TEETH

TONGUE

lip

chin

mouth

Throat

figure 6

2. hand : fingers :: foot : _____ Toe _____

3. leg : knee :: arm : _____ wrist _____

4. brain : head :: throat : _____ Tongue _____

5. eye : see :: nose : _____ breathe _____

6. tooth : teeth :: foot : _____ Feet _____

7. hear : ear :: smell : _____ nose _____

8. leg : foot :: arm : _____ hand _____

9. tongue : mouth :: stomach : _____ ? _____

10. stomach : food :: lungs : _____ air _____

Exercise d

Reading means using your brain, thinking. Not everything that you read is correct. Are these sentences about parts of the body TRUE or FALSE?

_____T_____ 1. We have five fingers on each hand.

_____F_____ 2. A man has four arms.

_____F_____ 3. A man sees with his ears.

_____F_____ 4. The plural of tooth is tooths.

_____T_____ 5. A man smells with his nose.

_____T_____ 6. A dog has four legs.

_____F_____ 7. A man hears with his mouth.

_____T_____ 8. We have five fingers on each foot.

_____T_____ 9. Our ankles are between our feet and our legs.

_____F_____ 10. The plural of foot is foots.

Rewrite the sentences above to make them true.

Exercise e

Look at the calendar (figure 7) and complete the paragraph.

figure 7

October

Sun.	Mon.	Tues.	Wed.	Thurs.	Fri.	Sat.
			1	2	3	4
5	6	7	8	9	10	11
12	13	14	15	16	17	18
19	20	21	22	23	24	25
26	27	28	29	30	31	

Dr. Brown's nurse looks at the appointment calendar for October. Dr. Brown is a very busy doctor. He has appointments, meetings, every day except (but not) on weekends. He will have appointments ___*23*___ days in October. Every Monday morning, he has a
31, 31st, 23, 23rd
meeting at the hospital. He has ___*4*___ meetings at the hospi-
4, 4th, 5, 5th
tal in October. On the third Wednesday of every month, Dr. Brown goes to Denver in the afternoon. He will go to Denver on October ___*15th*___. He has an appointment with Mrs. Black on the third Friday of October. The date will be October ___*17th*___. Dr. Brown has an appointment with Mr. Black two weeks later. He will see Mr. Black on October ___*31st*___.

Exercise f

Circle the correct answer.

1. Dr. Brown is a nurse.	TRUE **FALSE**
2. Dr. Brown has appointments on Saturdays.	TRUE **FALSE**
3. Dr. Brown has meetings on Mondays.	**TRUE** FALSE
4. One afternoon a month, he goes to Denver.	**TRUE** FALSE
5. Mrs. Black's appointment is on a Wednesday.	TRUE **FALSE**

PREPOSITIONS

We use these prepositions to show time.

in	months	Example: *in* January
	years	*in* 1984
	the afternoon	*in* June 1986
	the morning	
	the evening	
on	days	Example: *on* Monday
	month + day	*on* June 24th
at	noon	Example: *at* 6:00
	night	*at* 5:15
	_____ o'clock	

Special Expressions.

go **to**
have an appointment **with**

Exercise g

Complete the following paragraph with the correct prepositions.

I came to the U.S.A. _____*on*_____ August 24th. Now my life is very different. _____*in*_____ the morning, I wake up _____*at*_____ 7:30. I take a shower and eat breakfast quickly. Then I go _____*to*_____ school. My first class starts _____*at*_____ 9:00. _____*to*_____ noon, I eat lunch with my friends. I finish my classes _____*at*_____ 3:00 _____*in*_____ the afternoon. After classes, I usually go _____*to*_____ the cafeteria with my friends. We talk and laugh. _____*in*_____ the evening, I do my homework. I usually eat dinner _____*at*_____ 8:00 _____*at*_____ night. After dinner, I watch TV. Then I go _____*to*_____ bed. _____*on*_____ June I will begin to study at an American university. In four years I will return to my country with a degree.

Exercise h

Complete this paragraph.

Dr. Brown is a very busy doctor. He has appointments every day except on weekends. He will have appointments _*23*_ days _*in*_ 23, 23rd | in, on October. Every Monday morning he has a meeting at the hospital. He has _*4*_ meetings at the hospital _*in*_ October. On the _*third*_ 4, 4th | in, on | three, third Wednesday of every month, Dr. Brown goes _*to*_ Denver _*in*_ the to, on | in, on afternoon. He will go to Denver _*on*_ October _*15th*_. He has an in, on | 15, 15th appointment with Mrs. Black on the _*third*_ Friday _*of*_ October. three, third | in, on Dr. Brown has an appointment _*with*_ Mr. Black two weeks later. He with, on will see Mr. Black _*on*_ October _*31st*_. in, on | 31, 31st.

Look on page 19. How many mistakes did you make?

0 - 2 Excellent
3 - 5 Good
6 - 8 Fair
9 - 14 You need to study!

Exercise i

Complete the paragraph. Then answer the questions using the calendar (figure 8).

Dr. Johnson has a new nurse. Her name is Miss Smith. He tells Miss Smith to write his patients' names in his appointment book. He reminds her that he doesn't work on weekends. He says, "Mr. Taylor has an appointment on the _second_ Tuesday in June in the morning.
two, second
Mrs. Thompson is coming in the afternoon on June _FOURTH_. Miss
four, fourth
Roberts has an appointment in the morning _three_ days before Mr.
three, third
Taylor. I'm going to see Mr. Thompson in the afternoon a week after Mrs. Thompson. Mrs. Taylor is coming in the morning _two_ days
two, second
before her husband. Mr. Martin has an appointment in the morning on the _second_ Friday in June."
two, second

figure 8

June

Sun.	Mon.	Tues.	Wed.	Thurs.	Fri.	Sat.
1	2	3	4	5	6	7
8	9	10	11	12	13	14
15	16	17	18	19	20	21
22	23	24	25	26	27	28
29	30					

1. Who is Miss Smith?
2. What does Miss Smith write?
3. Where does Miss Smith write the names?
4. How many patients will Dr. Johnson see this month?
5. Who are Dr. Johnson's patients this month?
    a. *The new nurse.*
    b. *Dr's appointments.*
    c. *In the appointment's book.*
    d.
    e.
    f.
6. This is Dr. Johnson's appointment book. Can you help Miss Smith complete it?

Appointment Book

Mon.

June 2nd a.m. _____

         p.m. _____

Tues.

June 3rd a.m. _____

         p.m. _____

Wed.

June 4th a.m. _____

         p.m. *Mrs. Thompson*

Thurs.

June 5th a.m. _____

         p.m. _____

Fri.

June 6th a.m. _____

         p.m. _____

Mon.

June 9th a.m. _____

         p.m. _____

Tues.

June 10th a.m. *Mr. Taylor*

         p.m. _____

Wed.

June 11th a.m. _____

         p.m. _____

Thurs.

June 12th a.m. _____

         p.m. _____

Fri.

June 13th a.m. _____

         p.m. _____

APPOSITIVES

Usually a writer explains new words for you. He or she often uses punctuation to help you understand the new words. For example:

My sister, Maria, lives in Caracas.

Who is Maria? She is my sister.
Look at the commas (,   ,)

My sister, Maria, lives in Caracas.

The word between commas is the same as or tells about the word or words before the commas.

Many students from the Middle East don't like McDonald's hamburgers. They prefer to eat Kabsa (beef with rice).

What is Kabsa? Beef with rice.
Look at the parentheses ( ).

They prefer to eat Kabsa (beef with rice).

The words between the parentheses explain the word or words before the parentheses.

Exercise j

What word is the writer explaining in each of the sentences? What does the word mean?

1. Many students use a <u>bilingual</u>, two language, dictionary.
2. All of the students except (but not) Juan are looking at the blackboard.
3. People from Venezuela like to eat corn cakes (arepas).
4. My head aches, hurts. I need to take an aspirin (a pill).
5. I have a stomach ache (my stomach hurts).
6. The stomach, heart and lungs are internal organs, parts inside our bodies.
7. I can't walk because I twisted (turned) my ankle.
8. My mother and father have 6 children: 3 sons (boys) and 3 daughters (girls).
9. My cousins (my aunt's children) want to study in the U.S., too.
10. Most American families have pets, animals that live in the house.

Read this passage.

HELP MRS. BAXTER

Mrs. Baxter has a large family. She has 4 sons: Mark, Jim, Peter, and Sam, and 2 daughters: Mary and Janet. Unfortunately, all of her children need to see a doctor this month.

Mark needs a routine (regular) physical because he wants to play baseball at school. He needs to see Dr. Brown, the family doctor. Jim can't see the blackboard well, so he needs to see the eye doctor, Dr. Jackson. Peter has a toothache, so he made an appointment with Dr. Smiley, the dentist. Sam has red spots, a rash, on his face and chest. He will see Dr. Clearwater, the dermatologist. Mary has had a stomach ache for 10 days. She needs to see the internist, Dr. Burgess. Janet, the baby, has a bad cold. She needs to see Dr. Anderson, the pediatrician.

Mrs. Baxter is taking Janet to the children's doctor on the first Tuesday of the month at 11:00 a.m. Two days later, she made an appointment with Dr. Brown at 4:00 p.m. One week later, Peter has an appointment at 3:30 p.m. Three days before the appointment with Dr. Smiley, Mary will see the stomach doctor at 1:30 p.m. Two weeks after Janet's appointment, Sam will see the skin doctor at 10:00 a.m. On the last Friday of the month, Jim will see the ophthalmologist at 9:30 a.m.

Exercise k

Can you answer these questions without a dictionary? Look for commas.

1. What does *routine* mean? *There is a check up exam. Preventine*
2. What is a *rash*? *external allergie in your skin, red spots.*
3. What kind of doctor is a *dermatologist*? He is a ___*skin*___ doctor.
4. What kind of doctor is an *internist*? *Internal Medicine*
5. What kind of doctor is an *ophthalmologist*? *Eye Doctor*
6. What kind of doctor is a *pediatrician*? *Children doctor*
7. What kind of doctor is a *dentist*? *teeth doctor.*

Exercise I

Match the doctor's name with the kind of doctor.

_c_ 1. doctor for teeth problems   a. Dr. Anderson

_D_ 2. family doctor   b. Dr. Clearwater

_e_ 3. doctor for stomach problems   c. Dr. Smiley

_F_ 4. doctor for eye problems   d. Dr. Brown

_a_ 5. doctor for babies   e. Dr. Burgess

_B_ 6. doctor for skin problems   f. Dr. Jackson

Exercise m

Guess the answers. T = true   F = not true   ? = not enough information.

1. Mrs. Baxter will spend a lot of money this month.   T   F   **?**
2. Mark is 3 years old.   T   F   **?**
3. Jim has problems at school.   T   **F**   ?
4. Mrs. Baxter has 6 children.   **T**   F   ?
5. Jim has 3 brothers and 2 sisters.   **T**   F   ?

Exercise n

This is Mrs. Baxter's calendar (figure 9). Can you help her? Write the child's name, the time, and the doctor's name in the correct place on the calendar.

	Sun.	Mon.	Tues.	Wed.	Thurs.	Fri.	Sat.
						1	2
	3	4	5	6	7	8	9
	10	11	12	13	14	15	16
	17	18	19	20	21	22	23
	24	25	26	27	28	29	30

figure 9

3

The Family
Tree

PRONOUNS

Read the following paragraph.

Jim has a good friend at the university. The good friend's name is Bill. Bill is a business student. Jim and Bill are studying Business History and the Economics of Europe together this year. Business History and the Economics of Europe are difficult classes, but Business History and the Economics of Europe are very important. The teachers give a lot of homework. The homework is often very long and difficult. Jim is also taking Chemistry. Chemistry is a very difficult class for Jim. Bill is taking Business Math, but Business Math is an easy class for Bill.

Is this a good paragraph? No, it isn't a good paragraph because many of the words are repeated again and again. Writers use pronouns (*he, she, it, they,* etc.) so that they don't repeat the same words.

This is the same paragraph, but it uses pronouns. What do the italicized words mean? Look at the sentence before to find the meaning.

Jim has a good friend at the university. *His* name is Bill. Bill is a business student. *They* are studying Business History and the

Economics of Europe together this year. *They* are difficult classes, but *they* are very important. The teachers give a lot of homework. *It* is often very long and difficult. Jim is also taking Chemistry. *It* is a very difficult class for *him*. Bill is taking Business Math, but *it* is an easy class for *him*.

Exercise a

Read this paragraph and tell what these words mean.

Bob and Mary went to the grocery store last night. They go there at night because they work during the day. Bob went to the bread department, and Mary went to the fruit department. He got some bread. It was very fresh. She wanted some apples and oranges, but they were not good, so she did not get them. Then they went to the meat department. They asked the man there for some hamburger and some fish. He gave them the hamburger, but he didn't give them the fish because he didn't have any.

1. They (line 1)
2. there (line 1)
3. they (line 2)
4. He (line 3)
5. It (line 4)
6. She (line 4)
7. they (line 4)
8. she (line 5)
9. them (line 5)
10. they (line 5)
11. They (line 6)
12. there (line 6)
13. He (line 7)
14. them (line 7)
15. he (line 7)
16. them (line 7)
17. he (line 8)
18. any (line 8)

Exercise b

Read the paragraph and tell what the pronouns mean.

Mary studies at the library every afternoon. First, she looks at the grammar exercises. She reviews the incorrect answers. Then she rewrites them carefully. Second, she rereads the paragraphs from reading class carefully and slowly. They are often long and a little difficult. Finally, she begins to work on her writing homework. Sometimes she has an unsatisfactory paragraph, so she rewrites it. She is careful to change the incorrect words. After she studies, she goes to the cafeteria to drink something. Mary dislikes American coffee, so she drinks tea. She uses three spoonfuls of sugar in her tea to sweeten it.

1. she (line 1)
2. them (line 3)
3. They (line 4)
4. it (line 6)
5. it (line 9)

FAMILY MEMBERS

Exercise c

Alphabetize the following groups of words.

I	II
_____ parent	_____ father-in-law
_____ father	_____ mother-in-law
_____ mother	_____ sister-in-law
_____ child	_____ brother-in-law
_____ son	_____ son-in-law
_____ daughter	_____ daughter-in-law
_____ brother	_____ husband
_____ sister	_____ wife
_____ relative	

III		IV
_____ uncle		_____ grandparent
_____ aunt		_____ grandmother
_____ cousin		_____ grandfather
_____ nephew		_____ grandchild
_____ niece		_____ granddaughter
		_____ grandson

You have two parents: your mother and your father. The other people in your family are your relatives.

Exercise d

Look at this family tree (figure 10). Read the sentences and answer the questions.

figure 10

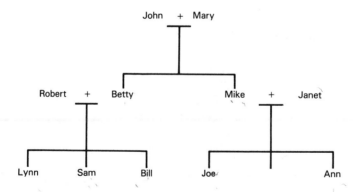

1. Mary is John's wife. Who is Robert's wife? ___*Betty*___
2. Robert is Betty's husband. Who is Janet's husband? ___*Mike*___
3. John is Betty's father. Who is Bill's father? ___*Robert*___

4. Mary is Mike's mother. Who is Ann's mother? _Janet_

5. Mary and John have two children. How many children do Robert and Betty have? _three (children) ?_

6. Betty is Mary's daughter. Who is Mike's daughter ? _Ann_

7. Sam and Bill are Robert's sons. Who is Mary's son? _Mike_

8. Betty is Mike's sister. Who is Joe's sister? _Ann_

9. Joe is Ann's brother. Who are Lynn's brothers? _Sam & Bill_

10. Betty is Joe and Ann's aunt. Who is Bill's aunt? _Janet_

11. Mike is Sam's uncle. Who is Ann's uncle? _Robert_

12. Joe has three cousins: Lynn, Sam, and Bill. How many cousins does Sam have? _TWO, Joe & Ann_

13. Sam and Bill are Mike's nephews. Who is Robert's nephew? _Joe_

14. Ann is Robert's niece. Who is Janet's niece? _Lynn_

15. Mary is Janet's mother-in-law. Who is Janet's father-in-law? _John_

16. Betty is Janet's sister-in-law. Who is Janet's brother-in-law? _Robert_

17. Robert is Mary's son-in-law. Who is Mary's daughter-in-law? _Janet_

18. John is Joe's grandfather. Who is Joe's grandmother? _Mary_

19. John has three grandsons. Who are they? _Joe, Sam & Bill_

20. John has two granddaughters. Who are they? _Ann & Lynn_

21. How many grandchildren does Mary have? _five_ Who are they? _Lynn, Sam, Bill, Joe & Ann._

FAMILY TREE

Exercise e

Choose one place on the family tree (figure 11) for yourself. Identify (tell) the other people, for example, my cousin, etc.

figure 11

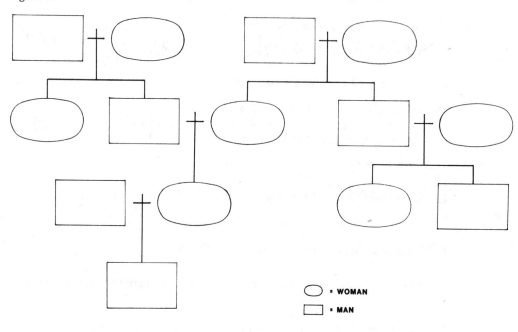

○ ▪ WOMAN

▢ ▪ MAN

Exercise f

Make your own family tree.

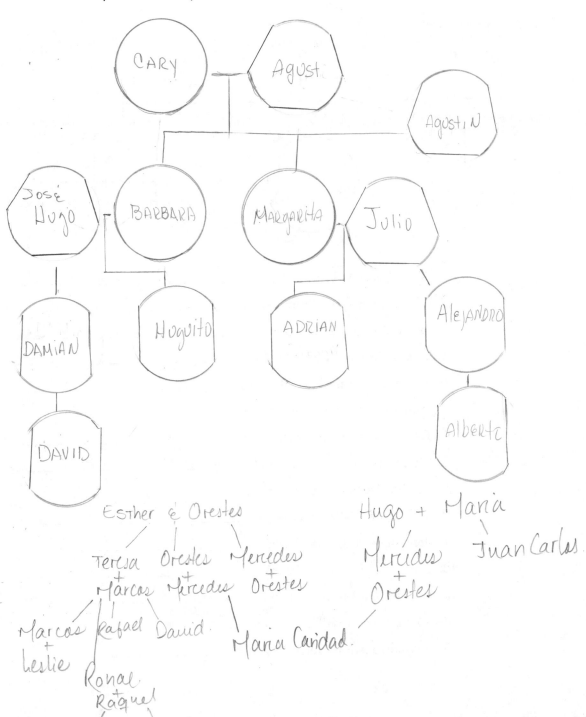

Esther & Orestes

Teresa   Orestes   Mercedes
+   +
Marcos   Mercedes   Orestes

Marcos   Rafael   David
+
Leslie   Ronal
          Ráquel
Gilliam   Rian

Hugo + Maria

Mercedes   JuanCarlos
+
Orestes

Maria Caridad.

Exercise g

Look at the following family tree (figure 12) and complete the sentences.

figure 12

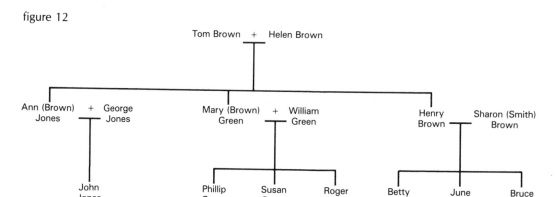

1. Mary Green is Phillip Green's _____ .

2. William Green is Phillip Green's _____ .

3. Betty Brown is Bruce Brown's _____ .

4. Henry Brown is Mary Green's _____ .

5. Henry Brown is Helen Brown's _____ .

6. Ann Jones is Tom Brown's _____ .

7. George Jones is Bruce Brown's _____ .

8. Sharon Brown is Phillip Green's _____ .

9. Phillip Green is Ann Jones' _____ .

10. June Brown is Mary Green's _____ .

11. John Jones is Susan Green's _____ .

12. Ann Jones is George Jones' _____ .

13. George Jones is Tom Brown's _____ .

14. Tom Brown is William Green's _____ .

15. Sharon Brown is Helen Brown's _____ .

Exercise h

Read the passage and complete the family tree (figure 13).

Jim Mason married Janet in 1936. They had three children: two daughters, Peggy and Sue, and one son, Steve.

Peggy married Dave Blake in 1956. They have one son, Bill.

Sue married Jeffrey Green in 1960. They have three children: two sons, Joe and Doug, and one daughter, Sharon.

Steve married Barbara Smith in 1958. They have three children: two daughters, Polly and Jean, and one son, Mark.

figure 13

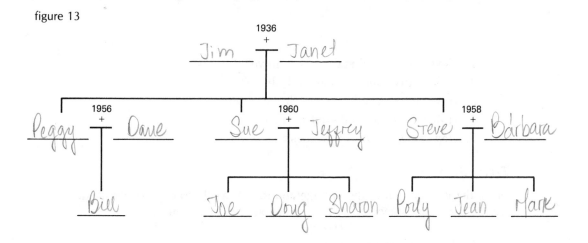

Exercise i

Read the following passage. Complete the family tree (figure 14) and answer the questions.

Mike Thompson married Susan in 1940. They had three children: two daughters, Ann and Barbara, and one son, Jim.

Their first child, Ann, married John Smith in 1963. They have one son, Robert, and two daughters, Betty and Mary.

Their second child, Jim, married Linda in 1969. They have one son, Tom.

Their third child, Barbara married Bill Brown in 1971. They have four children: one daughter, Sally, and three sons, Peter, Mark and Phillip.

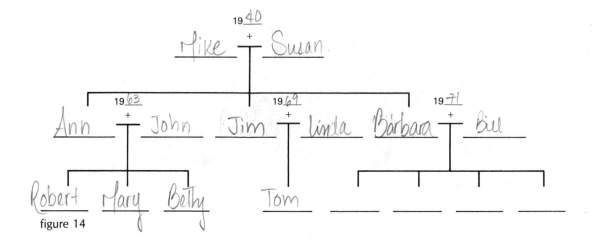

figure 14

1. How many cousins does Tom have?
2. How many cousins does Sally have?
3. How many grandsons does Mike have?
4. How many nieces does Jim have?
5. How many sons-in-law does Susan have?

Exercise j

**From the information in the passage and in the family-tree, *guess* the answers.
Yes = true   No = not true   ? = not enough information**

1. Ann is older than Jim.	YES NO ?
2. Tom is older than Mary.	YES NO ?
3. Jim is younger than Barbara.	YES NO ?
4. Mike and Susan have been married for more than 40 years.	YES NO ?

Exercise k

Read the following passage. Complete the family tree (figure 15) and answer the questions.

Mireya is a chemistry student at Stanford University, but her family lives in Venezuela. Her parents, Raul and Susan, live in Caracas. They have a large house and a large yard. Susan's mother, Isabel, lives with them. Susan takes care of the house and the children, and Raul is a lawyer.

Mireya's parents have two sons and two daughters. Mireya's older brother, Manuel, married Laura in 1970. They have three children: two sons, Tomas and Eduardo, and one daughter, Linda. Manuel and his family live in Maracaibo.

Mireya's younger brother, Daniel, is single. He is a teacher in Caracas. He lives with his parents.

Mireya's sister, Lucinda, lives in Barcelona with her husband, Luis. They have one daughter, Anita.

Mireya likes California, but she is unhappy because she can't see her family often. She wants to finish her degree quickly and return to Venezuela and her family.

figure 15

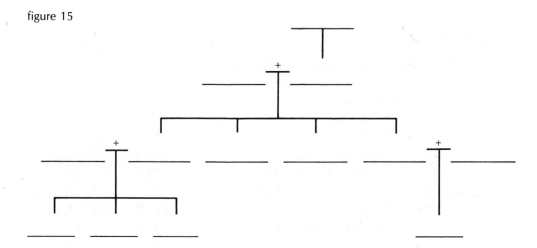

Exercise I

Answer the following questions.

1. How many children do Raul and Susan have?
2. How many of Mireya's relatives live in Caracas?
3. How many grandchildren do Susan and Raul have?
4. How many nieces does Mireya have?
5. How many nephews does Mireya have?
6. Who is Mireya's sister-in-law?

Exercise m

Give *three* answers to each question.

> Example: Who is Mireya? She is Susan's daughter.
> She is Manuel's sister.
> She is Eduardo's aunt.

1. Who is Linda?
2. Who is Lucinda?
3. Who is Raul?
4. Who is Laura?
5. Who is Isabel?

Exercise n

Are these sentences true or false or unknown?

1. Daniel isn't married.	TRUE	FALSE	?
2. Raul is Anita's grandmother.	TRUE	FALSE	?
3. Manuel is Luis's brother-in-law.	TRUE	FALSE	?
4. Linda is eight years old.	TRUE	FALSE	?
5. Isabel is Mireya's grandmother.	TRUE	FALSE	?
6. Susan doesn't have any sisters.	TRUE	FALSE	?
7. Linda is Lucinda's nephew.	TRUE	FALSE	?
8. Daniel is older than Lucinda.	TRUE	FALSE	?
9. Isabel's husband is dead.	TRUE	FALSE	?
10. Eduardo can visit his grandmother every day.	TRUE	FALSE	?

Exercise o

Look at the calendar (figure 16) and answer the questions.

1. There are _____ Mondays in June.

2. There are _____ days in June.

June

Sun.	Mon.	Tues.	Wed.	Thurs.	Fri.	Sat.
	1	2	3	4	5	6
7	8	9	10	11	12	13
14	15	16	17	18	19	20
21	22	23	24	25	26	27
28	29	30				

figure 16

3. My husband's brother has an appointment with Dr. Jones on the second Tuesday in June. My brother's son has an appointment with the doctor a week later. My father's wife has an appointment on June 24th. My mother's sister will see the doctor a week before my mother. When will my relatives see the doctor?

My brother-in-law will see the doctor on the ＿＿＿＿＿＿＿.

My aunt will see the doctor on the ＿＿＿＿＿＿＿＿.

My nephew will see the doctor on the ＿＿＿＿＿＿＿＿.

My mother will see the doctor on the ＿＿＿＿＿＿＿＿.

Animals

4

VOCABULARY FOR HOW ANIMALS MOVE

Exercise a

Alphabetize these groups of words.

I	II	III
_____ to jump	_____ wild animal	_____ wings
_____ to fly	_____ mammal	_____ fins
_____ to swim	_____ insect	_____ tail
_____ to crawl	_____ fish	_____ legs
_____ to climb		
_____ to walk		

Exercise b

Guess the meaning of the italicized words.

1. *Mammals*, animals with hair, live everywhere in the world. Cats and dogs are mammals.
2. People don't like *insects*, small animals with eight legs, because they often bite.
3. *Fish* can't walk. They *swim* in the water.
4. Cats can run fast and *climb* trees.
5. Before a baby can walk, he *crawls* on his hands and knees.
6. Birds don't have arms. They have *wings*, so they can *fly* fast.
7. Cats and dogs have four legs and a *tail*, but people have two arms and two legs and no tail. Fish don't have legs, but they have *fins* and a tail.
8. *Wild animals* don't live with people. Lions and tigers are examples of wild animals.

FINDING EXAMPLES

These words show us examples.

After the words   *such as*
                    like   we find examples.
                    for example
                    include

Exercise c

Look at the examples in the following sentences. The signal word (the word that tells the reader to look for an example) is circled. Underline the examples and answer the questions.

1. In some countries, (such as) *Mexico and Venezuela*, people speak Spanish.
   What is Mexico? It's a country where people speak Spanish.
2. In other countries, (like) Saudi Arabia, Iraq, and Yemen, people speak Arabic.
   What is Yemen?
3. In still other countries, (for example) Canada and Britain, people speak English.
   What is Britain?

4. English-speaking countries (include) Canada, Britain, and the United States.
What is Canada?

Exercise d

Complete the following examples.

1. Some animals, such as _____, can run fast.

2. Other animals, like _____, live in the water.

3. Some animals, for example _____, can fly.

4. Wild animals include _____ and _____.

5. _____ and _____ are examples of tame animals (animals that live with people).

Exercise e

Look at the following sentences. Circle the signal words in each sentence and answer the question.

1. Some wild animals, such as lions, tigers, and bears, have sharp teeth.
What are lions? Wild animals with sharp teeth.
What are tigers? Wild animals with sharp teeth.
What are bears? Wild animals with sharp teeth.

2. Some fish, for example trout, live in mountain rivers.
What are trout?

3. Some animals, such as snakes, crawl because they can't walk.
What are snakes?

4. Other animals, like fish and whales, live in the water.
What are whales?

5. Some birds, such as penguins, can't fly. They walk.
What are penguins?

6. Animals that live in people's houses, pets, include dogs, cats, and hampsters.
What are hampsters?

7. Some body parts, such as lungs and kidneys, are inside the body.
What are kidneys?

8. Certain people, like doctors and lawyers, study for many years before they can work.
   What are lawyers?

9. Many cities in Colorado, like Fort Collins and Steamboat Springs, are near the mountains.
   What is Steamboat Springs?

10. Some insects, such as butterflies and mosquitoes, can fly.
    What are mosquitoes?

11. Some animals, like deer, have very long legs, so they can run very fast.
    What are deer?

12. Other animals, such as kangaroos and frogs, can jump.
    What are kangaroos?

13. Some birds, such as robins and hummingbirds, can fly very fast.
    What are robins?

14. Some animals, such as rabbits and cows, are herbivores, plant-eating.
    What are rabbits?

15. Other animals, like man and dogs, are omnivores. They eat plants and meat.
    What are dogs?

Exercise f

Read the paragraphs and circle the examples you see.

HOW ANIMALS MOVE

All animals can move. Some move quickly. Some move very slowly. Some move in the air, but others move in the water.

Some animals can run very fast. For example, the deer has very long legs, so it can run very fast. Some animals, like the cheetah, (a wild cat) can run 70 miles per hour.

Some animals can jump. They have very strong back legs and small front legs so that they can jump. Animals that can jump include rabbits and kangaroos.

Some animals can fly. They have small legs and strong wings. Birds, such as the robin and the owl, can fly for long distances. Other animals can fly, too. Mammals, like the bat, can fly. Many insects, for example, the bee and the butterfly, also fly.

However (but), not all birds can fly. Some birds are very large, and they have very small wings. These birds include the ostrich and the penguin. The ostrich has very long legs, so it can run very fast. The penguin has small legs and wings, but it can swim very fast.

Animals that live in the water can swim under the water. They have no legs, but they have fins and a strong tail to help them swim. Animals that swim under the water include fish, such as the trout and the shark, and mammals, like the whale and the dolphin.

Some animals have no legs, for example the snake and the worm. Snakes and worms crawl on the ground or under the ground. They can't run, but they can move quickly.

Many animals can move in several ways. For example, ducks can fly and swim. Frogs can jump and swim. Some snakes, like the python, can crawl, swim and climb trees.

Exercise g

Answer these questions.

1. How many examples did you find?
2. What is a cheetah?
3. What is a python?
4. How does a python move?

Exercise h

Look at the pictures (figure 17). From the information in the paragraphs, guess which animal and which picture are the same. Write the name of the animal under the picture.

1. deer	6. owl	11. penguin	16. snake
2. cheetah	7. bat	12. trout	17. worm
3. rabbit	8. bee	13. shark	18. duck
4. kangaroo	9. butterfly	14. whale	19. frog
5. robin	10. ostrich	15. dolphin	20. python

figure 17

MAIN IDEA

The main idea is the most general idea in the paragraph.

Exercise i

Which word is the most general? Circle it.

1. car	2. cat	3. English	4. Japan
Ford	dog	language	Argentina
Chevrolet	animal	Arabic	Iran
Mercedes	bird	Spanish	country

Exercise j

Now look back at the paragraphs on pages 43-44.

In paragraph 1, what word do we see many times? <u>Move</u>
We see <u>move</u> 5 times. It is the most important word in the paragraph.
Which sentence is the most general? <u>All animals can move.</u>
The first sentence is the main idea in paragraph 1. The other sentences talk about <u>how</u> animals move.

Look at paragraph 2.

What is the most important word? _____

Which sentence is the main idea? _____

Look at paragraph 3.

What is the most important word? _____

Which sentence is the main idea? _____

Look at paragraph 4.

What is the most important word? _____

Which sentence is the main idea? _____

Look at paragraph 5.

What is the most important word? _____
Which sentence is the main idea? _____

Look at paragraph 6.

What is the most important word? _____
Which sentence is the main idea? _____

Look at paragraph 7.

What is the most important word? _____
Which sentence is the main idea? _____

Look at paragraph 8.

What is the most important word? _____
Which sentence is the main idea? _____

PREVIEWING

Before reading a long passage, it is a good idea to preview it, that is, look at it before you read it. When we preview, we do the following:

Read the title (the main idea).
Read the subtitles (the titles under the main title).
Look at the illustrations (pictures, graphs, etc.).

This information gives us a general idea about the information that is in the passage. It also gives us an idea about what is *not* in the passage.

You will practice previewing when you read the next passage, *Classifying Animals*.

VOCABULARY FOR CLASSIFYING ANIMALS

Exercise k

The italicized words in the following sentences are from *Classifying Animals*. Can you guess what they mean?

1. When I cut my finger, I see red *blood*.
2. Suliman is looking at Ali. Ali is looking at Suliman. They are looking at *each other*.
3. I have two brown shoes. I have a *pair* of brown shoes. I have two hands. I have a *pair* of hands.

The writer explains the following words in the passage. Look for them.

1. intelligent
2. fur
3. sets
4. limbs

Exercise l

Alphabetize these groups of words.

_____ hippopotamus   _____ lizard   _____ ant

_____ leopard   _____ crocodile   _____ fly

_____ elephant   _____ python   _____ butterfly

_____ monkey   _____ turtle   _____ mosquito

Exercise m

Can you match the word with pictures in figure 18?

Exercise n

Previewing activity. Look carefully at the picture for 2 minutes. Read the title and subtitles of the passage.

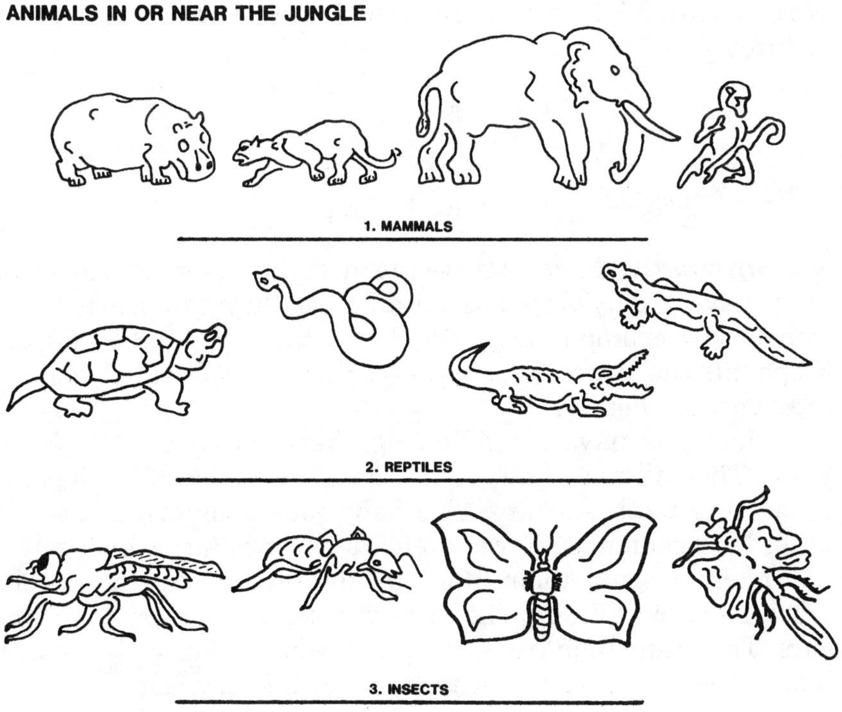

ANIMALS IN OR NEAR THE JUNGLE

1. MAMMALS

2. REPTILES

3. INSECTS

figure 18

Title: _____

Subtitles: _____

_____

_____

Exercise o

Now answer these questions.

1. How many kinds of animals will you read about?
2. What is one mammal you will read about? (Think of the picture.)
3. What is one reptile you will read about?
4. What is one insect you will read about?

We can learn a lot when we read the title and subtitles and look at the pictures.

CLASSIFYING ANIMALS

Mammals. Mammals are the most intelligent, or smart, animals. They have highly developed brains, so they can learn to do many things. For example, dogs can learn to help people who can't see. Elephants can learn to carry things. Some people think mammals can talk with each other.

Mammals have the following characteristics. They have warm blood. They all have hair, or fur, on their bodies. They have two sets (groups) of teeth and lips. The baby mammals drink their mother's milk. Most mammals have two pairs of limbs (arms or legs).

Mammals use their limbs in different ways. The antelope and zebra have long limbs. They can run fast. Monkeys have limbs like ours. They can climb trees. However, whales and seals have only two limbs. They can't walk, but they can swim very fast.

Mammals live everywhere. They live in very hot places and very cold places, like the North Pole. Hippopotamuses and monkeys live in the jungle. Elephants and leopards live near the jungle. Whales live in the water. Polar bears live in the North Pole.

Reptiles. Reptiles are another group of animals. Reptiles include snakes, lizards, turtles and crocodiles. All reptiles have cold blood. They breathe air with lungs like ours. They have scales on their skin. Baby reptiles come from eggs. Most reptiles have two pairs of limbs. Some reptiles have very short legs; however, others, like the snake, have no legs. All reptiles have these characteristics.

Some reptiles live in the jungle. Some reptiles live near the jungle. Others live in the mountains. However, reptiles do not live in very cold areas. Reptiles live everywhere except in cold places.

The most common reptile is the snake. There are many kinds of dangerous snakes in the jungle. One of these snakes is the python. The python is a huge (big) and powerful (strong) snake. It squeezes its food and then eats it. The python is sometimes 30 feet (about 9 meters) long. It can climb trees, swim in the water, and move on the land.

Insects. The insects are a very large group of animals. We know about thousands and thousands of insects, and every year people find more new insects. Insects live in all parts of the world. They live in the air, in the ground, and in fresh and salt water.

Adult insects have six legs. The body has three parts—head, middle section, and abdomen. There is a special liquid, or substance, on their skin. The head of an insect has eyes, mouth, and feelers. Baby insects come from eggs. All insects have these characteristics.

There are thousands and thousands of insects everywhere. Some examples of insects are flies, crickets, grasshoppers, moths, butterflies, mosquitos and ants.

Exercise p

What do these words mean?

    intelligent =

    fur =

    sets =

    limbs =

Exercise q

Write the paragraph number and the line number of the sentence that answers each of these questions.

1. What is on the skin of mammals?   Paragraph _____   Line(s) _____

2. How many limbs do most mammals have?   Paragraph _____   Line(s) _____

3. Where do mammals live?   Paragraph _____   Line(s) _____

4. What is on the skin of reptiles?   Paragraph _____   Line(s) _____

5. How many limbs do most reptiles have?   Paragraph _____   Line(s) _____

6. Where do reptiles live?   Paragraph _____   Line(s) _____

7. What is on the skin of insects?   Paragraph _____   Line(s) _____

8. How many limbs do   Paragraph _____   Line(s) _____
   insects have?

9. Where do insects live?   Paragraph _____   Line(s) _____

10. How many examples of   Paragraph _____   Line(s)_____
    mammals are there in
    the passage?

                              Paragraph _____   Line(s) _____

                              Paragraph _____   Line(s) _____

11. How many examples of   Paragraph _____   Line(s) _____
    reptiles are there in the
    passage?

                              Paragraph _____   Line(s) _____

                              Paragraph _____   Line(s) _____

12. How many examples of   Paragraph _____   Line(s) _____
    insects are there in the
    passage?

Exercise r

Complete this chart (figure 19)

Exercise s

Complete these sentences with information from the chart.

1. Mammals with two pairs of limbs include _____,
   _____, and _____.

2. Some mammals, like _____, live in the water.

3. Other mammals, such as _____, live near the jungle.

4. Snakes and lizards are examples of _____.

5. Some common insects are _____, _____, and
   _____.

	MAMMALS	REPTILES	INSECTS
LIMBS			
SKIN COVERINGS			
WHERE THEY LIVE			
EXAMPLES			

figure 19

Answer the questions.

6. What are three kinds of animals?

7. What are three characteristics of mammals?

Exercise t

Answer these questions. Read the directions carefully.

1. Underline the correct answer.

   _____ have fur on their skin.
   a. Mammals
   b. Reptiles
   c. Insects

2. Circle the correct answer.

   Snakes and turtles are _____.
   a. mammals
   b. reptiles
   c. insects

3. Check (✔) the correct answer.

   Insects have _____ limbs.
   a. 2 pairs of
   b. 4
   c. 3
   d. 3 pairs of

4. Circle the correct answers.

   Mammals live _____.
   a. in the water

  b. in the air

  c. on land

5. Fill in the blanks with the correct word.

| fly | insects | monkey | reptiles | substance |
| mammals | scales | snake | fur | |

There are many kinds of animals. Some are _____.

They have _____ on their skin. An example is a _____.

Others are _____. They have _____ on their skin.

An example is a _____. Still other animals are _____.

They have _____ on their skin. An example is a _____.

Exercise u

Are the following statements about mammals, reptiles, or insects?

  1. Have two sets of teeth. _____

  2. Live in the air, on land, and in the water. _____

  3. Live in both cold and hot areas. _____

  4. Live only in warm areas. _____

  5. Have scales on their skin. _____

  6. Have fur on their skin. _____

  7. Have six legs. _____

  8. Bodies have three parts. _____

  9. Babies drink their mother's milk. _____

 10. Have feelers on their head. _____

 11. Live on land and in the water. _____

 12. Warm-blooded. _____

 13. Highly developed brains. _____

 14. Babies come from eggs. _____

Exercise v

Complete this puzzle with words from *Classifying Animals*.

LINBS

ACROSS

4. Legs or arms
7. Animal with 6 legs
9. Reptile with short legs; very dangerous
11. Reptile with no legs
12. Baby mammals drink _____
13. Insects have _____ on their heads—not ears or nose

DOWN

1. Mammal living in the sea
2. Two
3. A kind of snake
5. A beautiful insect
6. An animal with scales is a _____
8. A reptile has _____ on its skin.
10. An animal with 2 sets of teeth
13. A mammal has _____ on its skin
14. Reptile and insect babies come from _____
15. Reptiles live everywhere _____ in cold places

figure 20

Across answers filled: 4. LIMBS, 7. INSECT, 9. CROCODILE, 11. FILES, 12. MILK. Down: 1. WHALE, 2. PAIR, 6. REPTILE, 13. FUR.

Exercise w

Read the following passage and circle the correct answer to the questions.

Most animals that live in the forests have small bodies. These animals can move quickly through the trees. They include the chipmunk, opossum, porcupine, raccoon, skunk, and squirrel. A few kinds of large animals, such as bear, boar, deer, and moose, also live there. The shores of the ponds, lakes, and streams of forests are the homes of the beaver, frog, muskrat, otter, salamander, and turtle. These animals live in the water and on land. Many birds, like the ovenbird and woodpecker, live in forests. They eat the insects and worms that live on the ground. Most forests are in Asia, Europe, and North America. Australia has some temperate forests where the echidna and the koala live.

1. An animal that lives both on land and in the water is
   a. the squirrel
   b. the otter
   c. the moose
   d. the woodpecker
2. The echidna lives in
   a. North America
   b. Asia
   c. Australia
   d. Europe
3. A small animal that lives in the forest is
   a. the boar
   b. the skunk
   c. the salamander
   d. the muskrat
4. The birds in the forests eat
   a. soil
   b. plants
   c. worms
   d. koala
5. The best title for this paragraph would be
   a. Large Animals
   b. Small Animals

    c. Animals that Live in the Forest

    d. Animals that Live in the Water

6. How many examples of large animals are in the passage?

    a. 4

    b. 2

    c. 6

    d. 15

Exercise x

Read the following passage and answer the questions.

Most animals that live in the mountains have small bodies. These animals can move quickly. Some examples are: chipmunk, opossum, porcupine, raccoon, skunk, and squirrel. Some large animals, such as the bear, the boar, the deer and the moose, also live in the mountains. Other animals, like the beaver, frog, muskrat, otter, salamander, and turtle, live in the water and on land. Many birds, for example the ovenbird and the woodpecker, live in the mountains. They eat the insects that live on the ground. There are many mountains in Asia, Europe, and North America. Australia has some mountains. The echidna and koala live there.

Circle the answer:

1. There are more large animals than small animals in the mountains.
   True   False

2. Birds and insects also live in the mountains.
   True   False

3. Name three animals that live on land and in the water.

    a.

    b.

    c.

4. Where does the koala live?

    a. In the water

    b. In the mountains in Australia

    c. In North America

    d. In the mountains in Asia

5. Do chipmunks and squirrels move fast?
   Yes   No

6. The main idea of this paragraph is
   a. Many large animals live in the mountains.
   b. Many small animals live in the mountains.
   c. There are many kinds of animals in the mountains.
   d. There are many kinds of animals in the water.

Foods

figure 21

Exercise a

There are many ways to classify (put into groups) foods. Look at these food circles (figure 21). Which of these circles shows the classification found in the passage *How the Body Uses Foods?* (You need to preview the article to answer this question.) The writer explains the following words in the passage, *How the Body Uses Foods.* Look for them.

1. wheat
2. oats
3. twice
4. beef
5. pork
6. goiter
7. night blindness
8. ascorbic acid

HOW THE BODY USES FOODS

There are many kinds of foods. They look, smell, and taste different. However, they are the same in one important way: they give our bodies what they need to live.

The human body uses foods in different ways. Some foods give us heat and energy. They are called carbohydrates and fats. Carbohydrates are fuel for the body like gasoline is a fuel for a car. Other foods help the body grow and repair itself. For example, many foods give proteins. Proteins help the body grow. They build muscles, skin and blood. Still other foods give us minerals and vitamins. They also help the body work well.

Carbohydrates Give Heat and Energy. There are two important kinds of carbohydrates. They are starches and sugars. Starches and sugars give the body heat and energy. The body uses the heat to stay warm. The body uses energy in almost everything people do. People need energy to move, talk, play, and study.

Starches and sugars are in many foods. Starches are in breads, spaghetti, rice, potatoes, and cereals such as wheat and oats. Sugar is in many fruits and other sweets, like honey, syrup, and candy.

Fats Also Give Energy. Carbohydrates are not the only energy foods. Fats give energy too. Fats give twice, two times, as much energy as sugars and starches. The body needs a long time to use energy from fats, so the body keeps the fat under the skin to protect the body.

There are two kinds of fats. Fats can be liquid, such as oils. Fats can be solids, like butter. Foods that have a lot of solid fat include bacon, cheese, peanuts, and cream.

Proteins Build the Body. Proteins are the most important builder in the body. The body needs protein to build all parts of the body. There are two kinds of proteins: complete proteins and incomplete proteins. Foods that have complete proteins include lean meats from cows (beef), pigs (pork), chicken and fish. Incomplete proteins are in foods such as nuts, peas, beans, and cereals.

Minerals: Another Builder. The body also needs minerals to build the body. One of these minerals is calcium. It helps to build strong bones and teeth. Calcium is in foods such as milk, cheese, eggs, and green leafy vegetables (vegetables with many green leaves).

Another important mineral is iron. It makes red blood cells. Everyone needs iron, but women and young children need more iron than others. Many foods, such as liver, egg yolk, beans, and leafy vegetables, have iron.

A third important mineral is iodine. It is necessary for the thyroid gland. If people don't get enough iodine, they can have a goiter (their thyroid gland grows too big.) Seafood, such as fish, lobster, shrimp and scallops, and iodized salt are examples of foods that have a lot of iodine.

Vitamins: Important Body Builders. Vitamins are very important for the body. There are more than thirteen kinds of vitamins. They help the body take the energy from foods, help the body grow, and help muscles work correctly.

Vitamin A is necessary for our eyes. People who don't have enough Vitamin A often have night blindness; that is, they can't see well when it is dark. Foods such as liver, eggs, milk, and cheese have a lot of Vitamin A. Green and yellow vegetables, such as broccoli and carrots, give the body carotene. The body can change carotene into Vitamin A.

Vitamin C, ascorbic acid, helps teeth and bones grow correctly. It also helps cuts heal, become better. Citrus fruits, like orange, grapefruits, and lemons, have a lot of Vitamin C. Other foods that give Vitamin C include tomatoes, broccoli, cantaloupe, and strawberries.

Our bodies need many things. There is not one food that has everything we need for heat, energy, growth, and repair. However, if we eat a balanced diet—some meat, some vegetables, some fruit, etc.—we can get everything our bodies need from food.

Exercise b

How did the writer explain these words?

1. wheat
2. oats
3. twice
4. beef
5. pork
6. goiter
7. night blindness
8. ascorbic acid

Exercise c

Underline the main idea in each paragraph.

Exercise d

Answer the following questions and tell where you found the answers (paragraph and line number).

1. How are foods different?
2. Name five things that foods give us.
3. Why does the body need sugar and starch?
4. Why does the body need fat?
5. Why does the body need protein?
6. Why does the body need calcium?
7. Why does the body need iron?
8. Why does the body need vitamins?

Exercise e

What do these pronouns mean?

1. They (paragraph 1 line 1)
2. They (paragraph 2 line 2)
3. They (paragraph 2 line 5)
4. They (paragraph 3 line 2)
5. It (paragraph 8 line 2)
6. It (paragraph 9 line 1)
7. It (paragraph 10 line 1)
8. they (paragraph 10 line 2)
9. They (paragraph 11 line 2)
10. they (paragraph 12 line 2)

OUTLINE

This passage, *How the Body Uses Foods*, is a classification. It divides the foods we need into different groups. Look at the following outline.

I. How the Body Uses Foods
  A. Foods that give heat and energy
    1. Carbohydrates
      a. Starches
      b. Sugars
    2. Fats
      a. Liquids
      b. Solids
  B. Foods that help the body grow and repair itself
    1. Proteins
      a. Complete
      b. Incomplete
    2. Minerals
      a. Calcium
      b. Iron
      c. Iodine
    3. Vitamins
      a. Vitamin A
      b. Vitamin C

This outline gives the main ideas in the passage. It does not use complete sentences or give any specific examples.

Exercise f

Answer the following questions by looking only at the outline.

1. What are the two ways the body uses foods?

2. How many kinds of food give heat and energy? What are they?

3. How many kinds of carbohydrates are there? What are they?

4. How many kinds of fats are there? What are they?

5. How many nutrients, kinds of food, help the body grow? What are they?

Exercise g

One way of remembering details from a classification passage is to make a chart.

Complete this chart (figure 22) from the information in the reading passage.

	SUGAR	STARCH	FAT	PROTEIN	IRON	CALCIUM	IODINE	VITAMIN A	VITAMIN C

NUTRIENTS

FOODS

figure 22

Exercise h

From the information in the outline and chart complete the following.

1. Some kinds of foods, such as _____, give you heat and energy.

2. Some foods, for example _____, give your body sugar.

3. Other foods, like _____, give your body starch.

4. Some foods, for example, _____, give fats to your body.

5. Some foods, such as meat and nuts, give the body _____.

6. _____ and _____ are good sources of fat.

7. Foods that give you calcium include _____ and

_____.

8. Some foods, _____ carrots and broccoli, give us Vitamin A.

9. Other foods, _____ oranges and grapefruit, give us Vitamin C.

10. Everyone needs Vitamin C to stay healthy. We do not want to get sick, so we eat foods that contain this vitamin. Two sources of it are

_____ and _____.

11. Our bodies need to stay warm: 98°F or 36°C. We get heat from foods that contain fats. These foods include _____ and

_____.

12. Young children and babies have growing bodies. They use a lot of protein each day. Some good foods for them to eat are

_____, _____, and _____.

13. Minerals are important in our diets. Our bodies need the calcium that is found in _____

14. Another important mineral, _____, makes the blood cells red.

15. Name five foods that contain sugar or starch. Alphabetize your answer.

   1.   4.

   2.   5.

   3.

Exercise i

Read the following paragraph and answer the questions.

There are four main kinds of meat: red meat, organ meat, fish, and poultry. Red meat includes meat from cows, pigs, and lambs. The most common kinds of red meat are beef (meat from adult cows), veal (meat from very young cows; that is, less than three months old), and pork (meat from pigs). The most popular kinds of pork include bacon, sausage, and ham. Lamb (meat from young sheep) is popular, but mutton (meat from adult sheep) is not popular in the U.S. Organ meats, such as liver, heart, kidneys, and brain, give a lot of minerals. There are three types of fish: salt water fish, fresh water fish, and shellfish, like lobster and clams. Poultry (birds) includes chicken, turkey, and duck.

1. Underline the main idea.
2. How many examples of organ meat are in the paragraph?
3. Are there examples of salt water fish in the paragraph?
4. Make a circle around the examples of poultry.
5. Make a rectangle (☐) around the words that signal examples.
6. Outline this paragraph.

Exercise j

Complete this puzzle with words from this chapter.

ACROSS

2. A and C are examples of _____
5. A favorite American dessert
6. A green vegetable that gives Vitamins A and C
8. A green leafy vegetable often used in salad
11. Lean meat gives complete _____
13. Fruit and candy give _____
15. Butter gives _____
16. A liquid fat
17. A product from chickens

DOWN

1. Rice gives the body _____

3. Iron is an example of a _____
4. _____ gives a lot of iron
6. A solid fat
7. A solid fat made from milk

9. An orange vegetable
10. Meat from cows
11. Meat from pigs
12. A citrus fruit
14. A product from cows

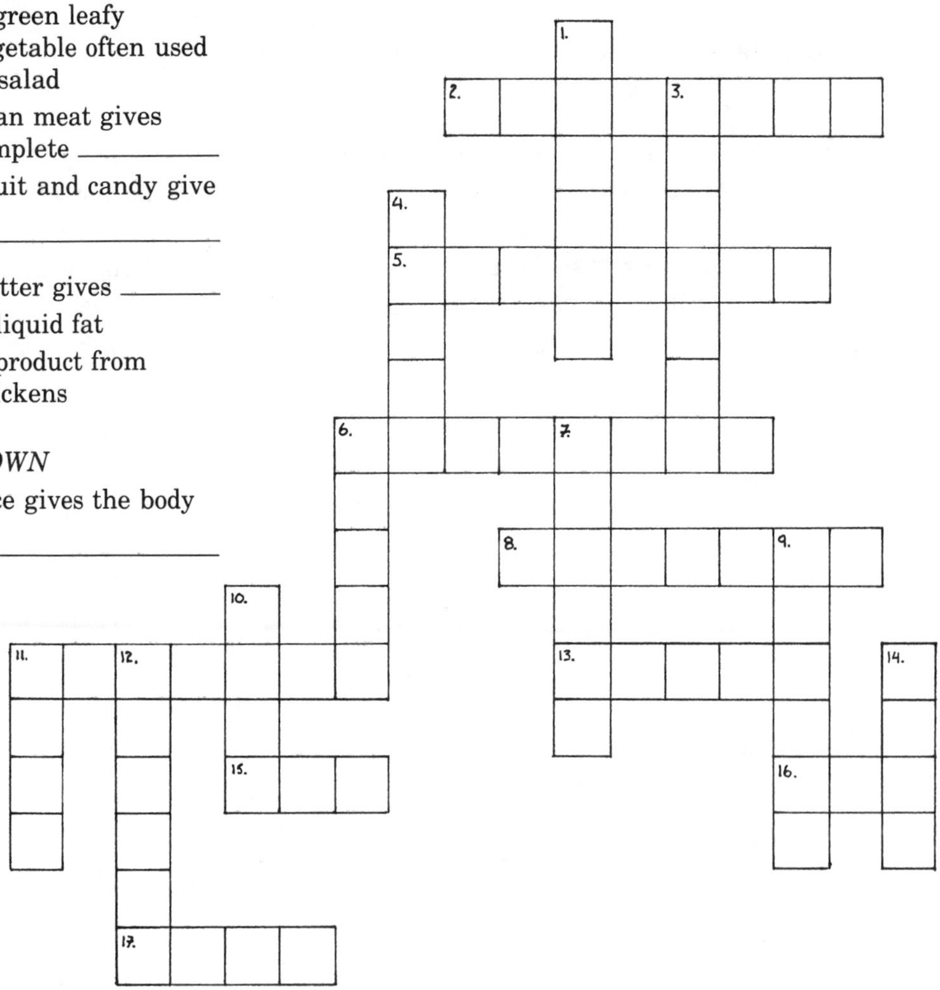

figure 23

Exercise k

Read this paragraph and answer the questions.

There are five important things in food: proteins, carbohydrates (sugar and starch), fats, minerals, and vitamins. The body uses proteins to build and repair its cells. Foods with a lot of protein include fish, eggs, meat, cheese, beans, and peas. The body can get energy from starches and sugars. Potatoes and bread have starch. Fruit has sugar. The body can also get energy from fat. A person can eat fat. We find it in foods such as butter, nuts, and fat meat. Minerals and vitamins are necessary for the body to work. We find minerals in nuts, milk, and vegetables. Foods like eggs, vegetables, and fruits have many important vitamins.

1. Underline the main idea in this paragraph.

2. Alphabetize the five things found in food.
   1.
   2.
   3.
   4.
   5.

3. The body uses _____ to build and repair cells.
   a. bread   c. apples
   b. eggs   d. butter

4. Fruits have _____
   a. vitamins   c. starch
   b. sugar   d. sugar and vitamins

5. We do *not* get energy from
   a. starches   c. fat
   b. vitamins   d. sugar

6. Circle the examples of proteins in this paragraph.

7. How many examples of foods with fats are in this paragraph? _____

8. Draw a rectangle around the words that show examples.

9. Outline this paragraph on your own paper.

Exercise I

Read the following paragraph and answer the questions.

Fruits and vegetables have lots of Vitamin A and Vitamin C. Vitamin C builds healthy gums and bodies. Vitamin A helps you see in the dark and have healthy skin. Many fruits and vegetables have lots of Vitamins A and C. Dark green and yellow vegetables are the best source of Vitamin A. Dark green vegetables include broccoli, collards, spinach, and turnip greens. Dark yellow vegetables include carrots, pumpkins, and sweet potatoes. Fruits like apricots and cantaloupe contain Vitamin A too. Oranges and grapefruit, called citrus fruit, have lots of Vitamin C. You can eat them fresh, or drink a glass of their juice. Strawberries, broccoli, and cantaloupe are high in Vitamin C as well. Cabbage and tangerines help with Vitamin C.

Circle the correct answer.

1. Broccoli, collards, and spinach are examples of
   a. dark yellow vegetables.   c. dark green vegetables
   b. fruits containing Vitamin C   d. fruits containing Vitamin A
2. How many examples of dark yellow vegetables are given?
   a. 3   c. 1
   b. 2   d. 4
3. Which two foods contain both Vitamin A and Vitamin C?
   a. oranges and grapefruit   c. cabbages and tangerines
   b. carrots and pumpkins   d. broccoli and cantaloupe
4. Apricots and cantaloupe are
   a. dark green vegetables   c. dark yellow vegetables
   b. fruits   d. citrus fruits
5. Underline the main idea of this paragraph.

6

Maps

DIRECTIONS

Following instructions (directions) is very important. Be sure to read each instruction carefully.

This is the vocabulary that you will need. See figure 24.

Exercise a

This is an exercise on following directions. Read each instruction and follow it carefully using your own piece of paper.

1. Write your name (last name first) in the upper right-hand corner.
2. Write the time under your name.
3. Write your mother's name at the bottom of this page.
4. Underline the first word in number 2.
5. Draw a rectangle in the upper left-hand corner.
6. Write the name of an animal inside the rectangle.
7. In the lower left-hand corner, write the names of your teachers.
8. Alphabetize the names of your teachers.

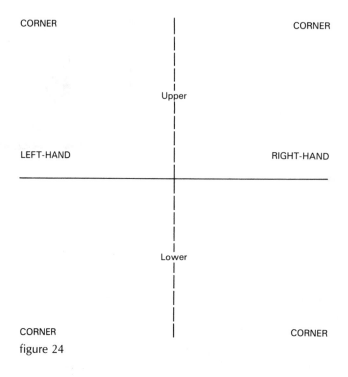

figure 24

9. Draw a triangle (△) around the name of your reading teacher.
10. Translate the following sentence into your native language: This exercise is easy. Write it in the lower right-hand corner.

Exercise b

Follow the directions carefully using a separate piece of paper.

1. Write your name in the upper left-hand corner.
2. In the upper right-hand corner, write your current address.
3. Under your address, write the date.
4. In the lower left-hand corner of this paper, write the names of three of your friends.
5. Translate the sentence "I like this class" into your native language. Write it under your name.
6. How many girls are there in this class? Write their first names in alphabetical order in the lower right-hand corner.
7. Make a circle around the third word in number 2.

8. Make a circle under number 9 and write three fruits in it.
9. Alphabetize these words.

_____ boat

_____ hate

_____ cat

_____ rat

_____ three

_____ catch

_____ late

READING MAPS

Following directions on a map is like following other kinds of instructions. First you need to understand some important instruction words, such as *north, south, east,* and *west.* Map makers always put *north* at the top of the map, or up, and *south* at the bottom, or down. *East* is on the right side and *west* is on the left side of the map. There are also directions that describe "up and to the right" (northeast), "down and to the right" (southeast) and others. The diagram below (figure 25) will be helpful to you when you read maps.

figure 25

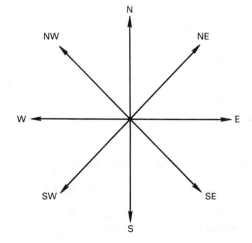

Exercise c

Look at the example and complete the analogies.

Example: Southeast : Northeast :: Southwest : *Northwest*

1. North : top :: South : _____

2. East : the right side :: West : _____

3. West : East :: South : _____

4. NE : SW :: NW : _____

5. Northwest : Southwest :: Northeast : _____

PREPOSITIONS OF PLACE

We use these prepositions to show place.

in +	cities	in San Diego
	states	in Florida
	countries	in Kuwait
	buildings	in the Chemistry Building
on +	streets	on South Main Street
	floors	on the third floor
	campus	on campus
at +	addresses	at 610 W. College Avenue
	places	at the blackboard

Exercise d

Complete the following paragraph with the correct prepositions.

I arrived _____ New York last week. Then I came here to learn English. I have a room _____ the dormitory _____ the fifth floor. I like living _____ campus because it is near the classrooms. My roommate is an American, so I

can speak a lot of English. My cousin is studying English
_____ London. He lives _____ a flat, an apartment, _____ High Street. His classes are _____
4610 Terry Road, so he takes the bus every day. He speaks English with
the other people on the bus.

Exercise e

Look at the map (figure 26) and complete the sentences.

figure 26

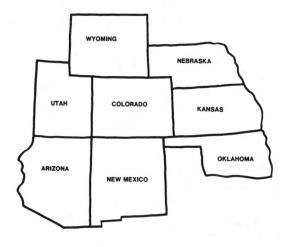

1. The state north of Colorado is _____.

2. The state east of Colorado is _____.

3. The state south of Colorado is _____.

4. The state west of Colorado is _____.

5. The state northeast of Colorado is _____.

6. The state southwest of Colorado is _____.

7. The state southeast of Colorado is _____.

8. The following states border (touch) Colorado: _____

_____.

Look at the map (figure 27) and answer the questions.

figure 27

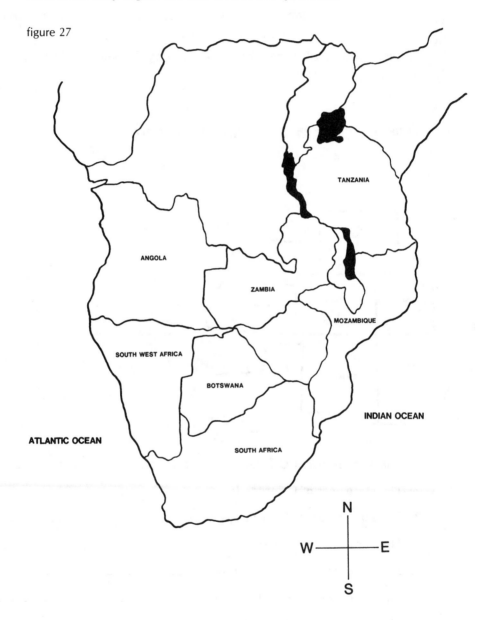

Exercise f

Complete the following sentences.

1. Botswana is ＿＿＿＿＿＿ of South-West Africa.

2. Zambia is ＿＿＿＿＿＿ of Botswana.

3. Angola is ＿＿＿＿＿＿ of Zambia.

4. South Africa borders ＿＿＿＿＿＿ countries. (How many?)

5. Tanzania is ＿＿＿＿＿＿ of Zambia.

Exercise g

Complete the map.

1. Zaire is northeast of Angola. Put Zaire on the map.
2. Zimbabwe is between Botswana and Mozambique. Put Zimbabwe on the map.
3. Malawi is to the east of Zambia. Put Malawi on the map.

Exercise h

True or false?

＿＿＿＿ 1. The Atlantic Ocean is to the east of Angola.

＿＿＿＿ 2. Mozambique borders 5 countries and the Indian Ocean.

Most maps have a scale of miles and/or kilometers. We can use the scale to find the distance (how far) between places. Look at the map on page 80. To find the distance from the Canadian border to Denver, Colorado, you need a small piece of paper. Put one edge (end) of the paper next to Denver. Make a mark on the paper where you see the Canadian border. Now put the piece of paper next to the scale.

How many miles is it? About <u>700</u> miles.
How many kilometers is it? About <u>1150</u> kilometers.
If we travel by car (average 55 miles per hour) how long will we travel? <u>12</u> hours.

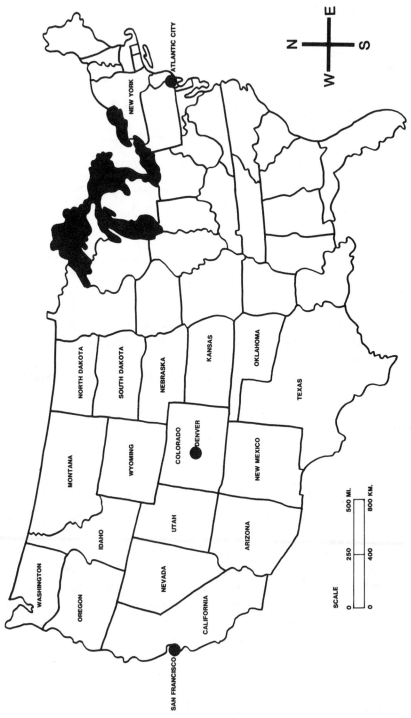

figure 28

Exercise i

Look at the map (figure 28) and answer the questions.

1. It is about _____ miles, or _____ kilometers, between San Francisco and Denver.

2. The state of New Mexico is _____ of Colorado. (Underline the correct answer.)
   a. north   c. east
   b. south   d. west

3. The geometric form of Colorado is a   (Circle the correct answer.)
   a. triangle   c. circle
   b. rectangle   d. octagon

4. There are _____ states whose borders touch Wyoming. (How many?)

5. The state that does *not* border Colorado is (Check the correct answer.)
   a. New Mexico   c. Oklahoma
   b. Utah   d. Texas

Exercise j

Look at the map (figure 29) and answer the questions.

1. It is about _____ miles, or _____ kilometers, between San Francisco and Atlantic City.

2. The state of Utah is _____ of Colorado.
   a. north   c. east
   b. south   d. west

3. The geometric form of Utah is a _____.
   a. rectangle   c. pentagon
   b. octagon   d. hexagon

4. There are _____ states whose borders touch Colorado.

5. The state that does not border the Pacific Ocean is _____.
   a. Washington   c. Oregon
   b. California   d. New York

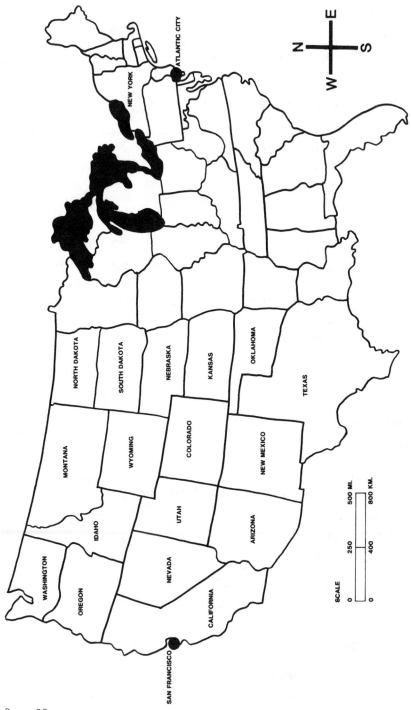

figure 29

Exercise k

Look at the map of Colorado (figure 30) and follow the directions.

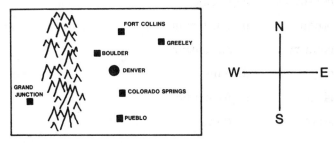

figure 30

1. Underline the name of the first city southeast of Boulder.
2. Circle the name of the city northwest of Greeley.
3. Make a triangle around the name of the city west of the mountains.
4. Make a rectangle around the name of the city north of Pueblo.
5. Alphabetize the cities on the map.
   1.
   2.
   3.
   4.
   5.
   6.
   7.

MAP READING VOCABULARY

There are 7 continents in the world. They are Africa, Asia, Australia, Antarctica, Europe, North America, and South America. Between continents there are oceans and seas. On each continent, there are many countries. For example, in Europe, we can find France, Germany, and Spain. In each country, there are cities, rivers (moving water), and lakes (nonmoving water). In the U.S., the country is divided into 50 states. The land that borders (touches) an ocean is a coast.

Exercise l

Match the following.

_____ 1. continent   a. Pacific

_____ 2. ocean   b. California

_____ 3. country   c. Argentina

_____ 4. city   d. Nile

_____ 5. river   e. Australia

_____ 6. state   f. Paris

We can say the same thing in different ways.

Canada *lies to the north of* the U.S.
Canada *is north of* the U.S.
Canada *is located (to the) north of* the U.S.

Exercise m

Make 10 sentences about your country using these expressions listed above.

Exercise n

Look at the map of the University campus (figure 31) and answer the questions.

figure 31

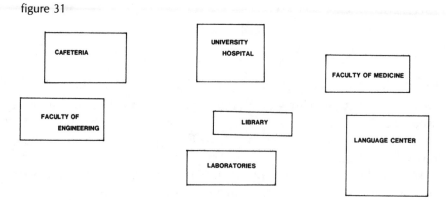

1. The _____ is located between the laboratories and the hospital.

2. The hospital _____ between the _____ and the _____.

3. The Faculty of Medicine _____ to the east of the hospital.

4. The _____ is located to the west of the library.

5. The hospital is located _____ the library.

6. The laboratories are located to the south of the _____.

7. The Faculty of Engineering is located _____ the cafeteria.

True or false?

_____ 1. The cafeteria is located in the center of campus.

_____ 2. The cafeteria is located to the west of the hospital.

_____ 3. The language center is located between the library and the laboratories.

_____ 4. The language center is located to the north of the Faculty of Medicine.

Exercise o

Look at the map (figure 32) and complete these sentences.

1. _____ and _____ are below (under) the Equator.

2. Sydney is _____ the Tropic of Capricorn.

3. Bangkok is below the _____.

4. _____ is above (over) the Tropic of Cancer.

5. Bangkok is _____ the Equator.

6. _____ is on the Tropic of Cancer.

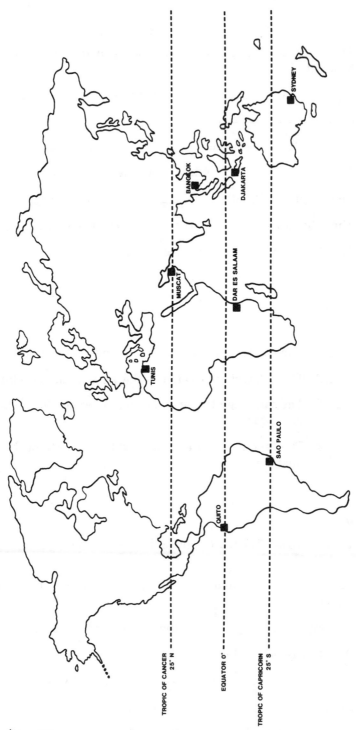

figure 32

7. Sao Paulo is _____ the Tropic of Capricorn.

8. _____ and _____ are between the Equator and the Tropic of Capricorn.

True or false

_____ 1. Djarkarta is above the equator.

_____ 2. Quito is on the Tropic of Cancer.

Exercise p

Read the passage carefully. Complete the map (figure 33) with the names of countries, states, rivers, and oceans.

THE U.S.A.

The United States is a large country. The Atlantic Ocean is to the east of the U.S. The Pacific Ocean is to the west. Canada is the country to the north. Mexico is the country to the south. The Caribbean Sea is also to the south.

On the Pacific Ocean, California has the longest coast. North of California is Oregon. The Columbia River is the border between Oregon and Washington. From west to east, Washington, Idaho, Montana, North Dakota, and Minnesota border on Canada. Minnesota also borders on Lake Superior. East of Minnesota is Wisconsin. Upper Michigan is northeast of Wisconsin. It borders on Lake Superior and Lake Michigan. Illinois and Indiana also border on Lake Michigan. Lower Michigan is between Lake Michigan and Lake Huron. East of Indiana is Ohio. The northern border of Ohio is Lake Erie. Pennsylvania is east of Ohio. New York is north of Pennsylvania. New York also borders on Lake Ontario and Canada. The states of Vermont, New Hampshire, and Maine border on Canada.

From north to south on the Atlantic Ocean are: Maine, New Hampshire, Massachusetts, Rhode Island, Connecticut, New York, New Jersey, Delaware, Maryland, Virginia, North Carolina, South Carolina, Georgia, and Florida.

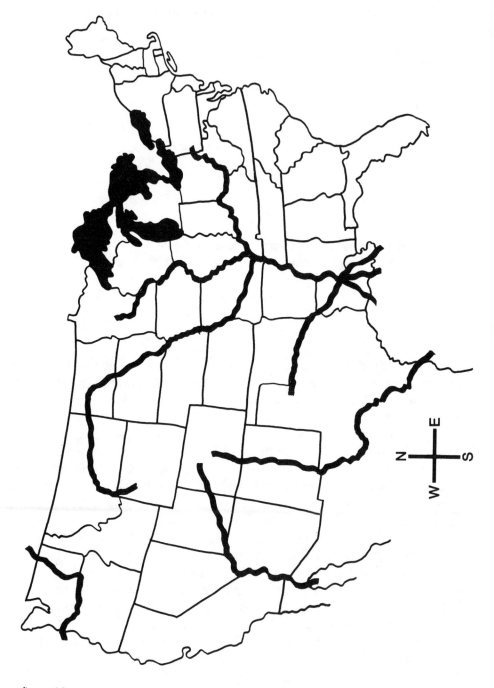

figure 33

The following states border on the Caribbean Sea from east to west: Florida, Alabama, Mississippi, Louisiana, and Texas.

There are many rivers that also are borders between states. The Rio Grande River is the border between Mexico and Texas. The Rio Grande starts in Colorado. Then it goes through the middle of New Mexico. The Colorado River also starts in Colorado. Then it goes west through Utah and into Arizona. It is part of the border between Nevada and Arizona. The Colorado River is also the border between California and Arizona.

The biggest river in the U.S. is the Mississippi River. It starts in Minnesota and ends in Louisiana. It is part of the border between Minnesota and Wisconsin. Many other states border this great river. On the east side of the river from north to south are Wisconsin, Illinois, Kentucky, Tennessee, and Mississippi. Along the west side from north to south are Iowa, Missouri, Arkansas, and Louisiana.

Two rivers join the Mississippi River; one comes from the west, the Missouri River, and the other comes from the east. It is the Ohio River. The Missouri River starts in Wyoming. Then it goes through North Dakota and South Dakota. It is the border between Nebraska and Iowa, and between Kansas and Missouri.

The Ohio River starts in Pennsylvania. It forms the southern borders of Ohio, Indiana, and Illinois. It is the northern border of West Virginia and Kentucky.

The last river on the map begins in Texas. It is called the Red River. It forms the border between Texas and Oklahoma. Then it goes into Louisiana and joins the Mississippi River.

Exercise q

Now complete these sentences.

1. Two states with almost the same shape are _____ and

_____.

2. Four states come together at the "Four Corners." There is only one place on the map where four states touch borders. These states are:

_____, _____, _____ and

_____.

3. The _____ River goes north before it goes south.

Exercise r

Answer these questions

4. How many states touch the Pacific Ocean?

5. Which states do not touch an ocean, river, or lake?

6. How many states have *new* in the names? What are they?

7

Textbooks

Read this passage and answer the questions.

THE PARTS OF A TEXTBOOK

Many of you will be reading textbooks in your classes. Most textbooks have the following parts: title page, introduction, table of contents, chapter titles and subtitles, illustrations, a glossary, and an index.

The title page is at the front of the book. The title page of a textbook gives the title of the book, the author, writer, and the place and date of publication. This information is very important if you are preparing footnotes or a bibliography, a list of books you read.

The introduction to the textbook usually follows (comes after) the title page. The author writes the introduction to explain the purpose of the textbook and often suggests how best to use the book.

The table of contents (sometimes called contents) usually follows the introduction. It lists, gives in writing, the titles of all the chapters, and it gives the page on which each chapter begins. The table of contents gives a general idea about the information in the text.

Each chapter in the text has a title, which is the main idea of the chapter. In addition, it probably has subtitles. Subtitles show the main idea of a group of paragraphs.

The illustrations in a textbook are very important. The author uses illustrations, such as graphs, charts, and pictures, to help explain his or her ideas. They are not used to make the book more interesting.

Many textbooks have a glossary at the end of the book. A glossary is a small dictionary of the technical, special, words that the author has used in the book.

The index is usually the last part of the textbook. It is arranged alphabetically. An index lists the important facts, places, people, etc. and tells on exactly what page(s) they are found.

Each of these parts of a textbook can help you find information efficiently, quickly and well.

Exercise a

Answer the questions.

1. The writer explains these words. What do they mean?
   a. bibliography
   b. list
   c. follow
   d. technical
   e. glossary
   f. efficiently
   g. author
2. How many examples of illustrations are given in the passage?
3. What do these pronouns refer to?
   a. It (paragraph 4 line 2)
   b. it (paragraph 5 line 2)
   c. It (paragrah 8 line 1)
   d. they (paragraph 8 line 3)

Exercise b

Complete this outline of *The Parts of a Textbook*.

I. _____
   A. Title Page.

    1. Location: _____

    2. Information: _____

    3. Importance: _____

B. Introduction

    1. Location: _____

    2. _____

    3. _____

C. _____

    1. Location: _____

    2. _____

    3. _____

D. _____

    1. title = _____

    2. subtitle = _____

E. _____

    1. Importance: _____

    2. Examples: _____

F. Glossary: _____

    1. Location: _____

    2. Information: _____

G. _____

    1. Location: _____

    2. Information: _____

    3. Organization: _____

Exercise c

Look at the outline and answer the following questions.

    1. What are the main parts of a textbook?
    2. Why is the title page important?
    3. Why is the introduction important?

4. Why is the glossary useful?

5. What information does the table of contents give you?

6. Order the following parts of a textbook. Which is first in the book? Which is second, etc.?

_____ Index

_____ Title Page

_____ Table of Contents

_____ Glossary

_____ Introduction

PREVIEWING

Before reading a chapter from a textbook, it is a good idea to preview (look before you read). When we preview, we do the following. We look at the title, subtitles, and the illustrations. This information gives us a general idea about the information in the chapter. If we have an idea about the information we will read about (and won't read about), it is easier to read and understand the chapter.

For example, when you preview a chapter you find:

Title	Meats
Subtitles	Beef
	Pork
	Poultry

From this information, answer these questions.

Will you read about hamburger?
Will you read about chicken?
Will you read about lamb?
Will you read about fish?

You will probably read about hamburger because it is a kind of beef, and one of the subtitles is "Beef." Chicken is a kind of poultry, so you will probably read about it, too. You will not read about lamb or fish because they are not kinds of beef, pork, or poultry.

Exercise d

Look at the following titles and subtitles. Is the answer to the question in the chapter? If yes, under which subtitle?

Animals that Migrate

Mammals
Birds
Fish

1. Do bears migrate?   YES   NO   SUBTITLE _____

2. Do snakes migrate?   YES   NO   SUBTITLE _____

3. Which fish migrate?   YES   NO   SUBTITLE _____

Important European Cities

London
Paris
Rome

4. Why is New York City important?   YES   NO   SUBTITLE _____

5. Where is Rome?   YES   NO   SUBTITLE _____

6. How many people live in Paris?   YES   NO   SUBTITLE _____

The State of Florida

Population
Climate
Natural Resources

7. How many people live in Florida?   YES   NO   SUBTITLE _____

8. What is the history of Florida?   YES   NO   SUBTITLE _____

9. Is there any oil in Florida?   YES   NO   SUBTITLE _____

TABLE OF CONTENTS

The table of contents is at the beginning of a textbook. It shows the organization of the book. For example, it shows the number of chapters and how many pages are in each chapter. The table of contents can help readers have a general idea of the information included in the book. Look at the table of contents below.

VITAMINS AND THEIR USES

TABLE OF CONTENTS

Exercise e

Answer these questions from the table of contents above.

1. How many chapters are in this book? _____

2. How many pages are in this book? _____

3. Can you read about the importance of Vitamin D? _____
   On what page(s)? _____

4. Can you read about the sources of Vitamin C? _____
   On what page(s)? _____

5. Can you read about minerals in this book? _____

6. Can you read about carbohydrates in this book? _____

7. Can you read about the uses of Vitamin A? _____
   On what page(s)? _____

8. Can you read about vitamin pills? _____
   On what page(s)? _____

9. How many pages are in Chapter 3? _____

10. How many pages are in Chapter 6? _____

11. On what page can you read about the importance of vitamin B_6?
    a. page 24   b. page 65   c. I don't know

12. On what page can you read about carotene, one of the sources of Vitamin A?
    a. page 19   b. page 23   c. I don't know

The table of contents gives us a general idea about the information in a book. In this book, we can read about Vitamins A, B, C, D, E, and K, but we can't read about minerals or carbohydrates. The answers to questions 11 and 12 above are probably in the book, but the table of contents can't tell us exactly where the information is located.

INDEX

If we want or need very specific information, such as the answers to questions 11 and 12, we can look in the index in the back of the book. The index shows on exactly which page we can find the information.

The information in an index is arranged, organized, alphabetically. The punctuation is very important. A comma (,) between page numbers means that the word can be found on the pages shown. A dash (–) between numbers means that the information begins on the first page number shown and finishes on the last page number shown. For example, *Carrots 89, 91* means that carrots are on page 89 and page 91. *Vitamin A 89–91* means that Vitamin A is on pages 89, 90, and 91.

VITAMINS AND THEIR USES

INDEX

Exercise f

Look at the index on the preceding pages and answer the questions.

When you are looking for specific information, it isn't necessary to read everything. The index is organized alphabetically, so you can find the information you need to answer the questions very quickly. This kind of reading is called scanning.

1. On what page(s) can you read about carotene? _____

2. On what page(s) can you read about lemons? _____

3. On what page(s) can you read about the importance of Vitamin B_6?

   _____

4. On what page(s) can you read about the kinds of vitamin pills?

   _____

5. On what page(s) can you read about the uses of Vitamin B_2?

   _____

6. On what page(s) can you read about riboflavin? _____

7. On how many page(s) can you read about the importance of vitamins
   in repairing cells? _____

8. On what page(s) can you read about calcium? _____

9. On what page(s) can you read about zinc? _____

10. Can you read about color blindness in this book? _____

AFFIXES

Affixes are groups of letters that are put before a word (prefix) and/
or after a word (suffix). These affixes change the meaning or the grammar, part of speech, of the word. By learning these affixes, you can
increase your vocabulary.

PREFIXES
We put prefixes before a word to change the meaning of the word.

Prefix	Meaning	Examples
re-	again	reread, rewrite, review, rebuild
un-	not	unhappy, unusual, unsatisfactory
dis-	not	dislike, disagree, dishonest
in-	not	incorrect, incomplete, incredible
pre-	before	preview, prefix, precook, pretest

SUFFIXES
We put suffixes after a word to change its meaning or part of speech:
noun, verb, adjective, adverb.

Suffix	Meaning	Examples
-er	person who (N)	teacher, learner, writer, reader
-en	to make (V)	shorten, sweeten, weaken
-ly	adverb (answers question: HOW)	slowly, quickly, usually, sadly
-ful	full of	spoonful, beautiful, wonderful
-ness	noun	sadness, happiness, illness

Exercise g

Circle the prefix and suffix and match the following.

_____	1. uninteresting	a.	full of beauty
_____	2. worker	b.	adverb of happy
_____	3. happily	c.	not interesting
_____	4. illness	d.	noun of ill
_____	5. beautiful	e.	to make short
_____	6. shorten	f.	person who works
_____	7. incorrect	g.	not agree
_____	8. review	h.	look again
_____	9. disagree	i.	look before
_____	10. preview	j.	not correct

Exercise h

Complete these sentences with words from the list.

disagrees   unhappy   rewrite   unsatisfactory

I am very _____, sad. I think my paragraph is very good, but
the writing teacher _____. She wants me to _____
the paragraph because it is _____.

slowly   sweeten   spoonfuls

I put two _____ of sugar in my coffee to _____ it. I
drink my coffee _____ because it is very hot.

Exercise i

Complete the following.

A person who reads is a _____.

A person who writes is a _____.

A person who works is a _____.

Exercise j

Complete the following chart (figure 34) by adding or removing the suffix.

Adjective	Adverb (-ly)	Noun (-ness)
bad		
	easily	
		happiness
	loudly	
quiet		
weak		

figure 34

Exercise k

Complete the sentences with the correct form of the word.

1. It is an _____ test. (easy)

2. He answers the question _____. (easy)

3. He hears a _____ noise. (loud)

4. He sings _____. (loud)

5. People should talk _____ in the library. (quiet) They shouldn't talk _____. (loud)

6. The _____ man can't pick up the chair. (weak)

7. The child plays _____ with the new toy. (happy)

8. The _____ boy hits his sister every day. (bad)

Exercise l

Complete the following chart (figure 35) by adding or removing the suffix.

Adjective	Adverb (-ly)	Noun (-ness)	Verb (-en)
sweet			
	sadly		
		darkness	
			sharpen
short			

figure 35

Exercise m

Complete the sentence with the correct form of the word.

1. He puts sugar in his coffee because he likes _____ coffee. (sweet)

2. He _____ his coffee with sugar. (sweet)

3. Many children are afraid of the _____. (dark)

4. Before the test, he _____ his pencil. (sharp)

5. Last year dresses were long. Now they are much shorter. I have to _____ my old dresses. (short)

6. It is a very _____ story. (sad) The story _____
   me. (sad)

Exercise n

Read this paragraph. Underline the words in the paragraph that have prefixes. Circle the words with suffixes.

Mary studies at the library every afternoon. First she looks at the grammar exercises. She reviews the incorrect answers. Then she rewrites them carefully. Second she rereads the paragraphs from reading class carefully and slowly. They are often long and a little difficult. Finally, she begins to work on her writing homework. Sometimes she has an unsatisfactory paragraph, so she rewrites it. She is careful to change the incorrect words. After she studies, she goes to the cafeteria to drink something. Mary dislikes American coffee, so she drinks tea. She puts three spoonfuls of sugar in her tea to sweeten it.

How many words did you underline?
How many words did you circle?

Exercise o

Follow the directions carefully using your own piece of paper.

1. Write your name in the upper right-hand corner.
2. Write two words with the *-er* suffix in the upper left-hand corner.
3. Write your telephone number under question 10.
4. Write two words with the *re-* prefix under your name.
5. Under your telephone number, make a circle and a triangle.
6. Draw a rectangle in the circle.
7. Write the time under the triangle.
8. Translate "This test is easy" into your native language. Write it in the lower right-hand corner.
9. Write the date in the left-hand corner.
10. Write two words with the *un-* prefix under the circle.

Exercise p

Read the directions and do what is asked on another piece of paper.

1. Write your name in the upper left-hand corner.
2. Write two words with the *-er* suffix under your name.
3. Write the name of your grammar teacher in the lower right-hand corner.
4. Underline the word in number 3 that has a suffix.
5. Make a circle in the upper right-hand corner.
6. Write the names of three fruits in the circle.
7. Write three words with the *re-* prefix in the lower left-hand corner.
8. Alphabetize the words with the *re-* prefix.

Temperatures and Other Measurements

Read the following passage.

READING A THERMOMETER

There are thermometers in every house. When we are very hot or very cold, we always want to know what the temperature is, so we look at a thermometer.

People in the U.S. use the Fahrenheit thermometer, but people in other countries use the Celsius, Centigrade, thermometer. We use the abbreviation F for Fahrenheit and C for Celsius and Centigrade.

When the temperature gets warmer, a little hotter, the mercury, the colored liquid in the thermometer, goes up, rises. This shows that the temperature is increasing. We can say that the temperature is rising, increasing, or going up.

When the temperature becomes cooler, a little colder, the mercury drops, goes down. This shows that the temperature is decreasing. We can say that the temperature is dropping, decreasing, or going down.

Look at thermometer number 1 in figure 36. There are numbers and lines on the thermometer. These lines are called degree lines. They are above (over) zero (0) and below (under) zero. The temperature on thermometer number 1 is 10 degrees above zero (10°). On thermometer number 2, also in figure 36, the temperature is 10 degrees below zero (−10°).

There are several temperatures that you should know in both Celsius and Fahrenheit. They are: freezing point, boiling point, and normal body temperature.

On the Fahrenheit thermometer, 32 degrees above zero is the freezing point. On the Celsius thermometer, the freezing point is zero degrees. At the freezing point, water changes into ice.

On the Fahrenheit thermometer, two hundred twelve degrees is the boiling point. The boiling point is one hundred degrees on the Celsius thermometer. At the boiling point, water changes into gas.

On the Fahrenheit thermometer, the normal body temperature is ninety-eight degrees. The normal body temperature on the Celsius thermometer is thirty-six degrees. It is very important to know if we are talking about the Fahrenheit or Celsius thermometer.

figure 36

THERMOMETER 1

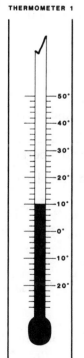

THERMOMETER 2

Exercise a

The writer explains these words in the passage. What do they mean?

1. Celsius (What is another word for it?)
2. warmer
3. mercury
4. rises
5. cooler
6. drops
7. above
8. below

Exercise b

Answer the following questions.

1. How do we know if the temperature is going up?
2. How do we know if the temperature is going down?
3. Why is it important to know if a temperature is Fahrenheit or Celsius?

Exercise c

Look at the thermometers (figure 37) and complete the following.

1. Look at thermometer number 3. Some of the lines are long, and some of the lines are short. Numbers are next to the _____ lines. If we move from one long line to the next long line, the temperature changes _____ degrees. If we move from one short line to the next short line, the temperature changes _____ degrees.
2. Thermometer number 3 shows that the temperature of the room is _____. This is a nice indoor temperature for us.
3. What is the temperature on thermometer 4? _____ This is the _____ point on the Celsius thermometer.
4. Thermometer number 5 shows _____. This is the _____ point on the Fahrenheit thermometer.

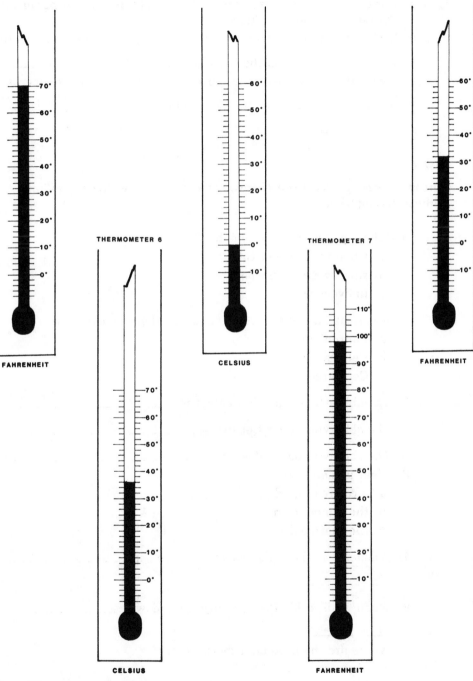

figure 37

5. If the temperature dropped to −20°F, would this be warmer or colder than 0°C? How do you know?

6. Look at thermometer number 6. What is the temperature? _____ On the Celsius thermometer, this is the _____.

7. Look at thermometer number 7. What is the temperature? _____ On the Fahrenheit thermometer, this is the _____.

Exercise d

Reread the passage *Reading a Thermometer*. Then answer these questions without looking back.

1. Where do we see thermometers?
   a. when we are very cold
   b. when we are very hot
   c. in every home

2. Americans use the _____ thermometer.
   a. Fahrenheit
   b. Celsius
   c. Centigrade

3. The abbreviation for Fahrenheit is _____.

4. The abbreviation for Celsius is _____.

5. The abbreviation for degrees is _____.

6. What is mercury?
   a. a colored liquid
   b. the temperature
   c. the thermometer

7. When it is hot, the mercury goes up, _____, or _____.

8. When it is cold, the mercury goes down, _____, or _____.

9. Where are the lines on a thermometer?
   a. above zero
   b. below zero

      c. above and below zero

10. What is the freezing point on the Fahrenheit thermometer?

      a. 32 degrees

      b. zero degrees

      c. ten degrees below zero

11. What is the boiling point on the Celsius thermometer?

      a. 212 degrees

      b. 100 degrees

      c. zero degrees

12. The normal body temperature is _____°F or _____°C.

figure 38

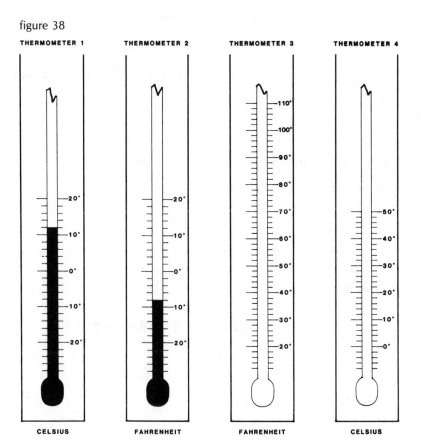

Exercise e

Look at these thermometers (figure 38) and answer the questions.

1. What is the temperature on thermometer number 1? _____
2. What is the temperature on thermometer number 2? _____
3. Draw the mercury on thermometer number 3 to read the normal body temperature in degrees Fahrenheit.
4. Draw the mercury on thermometer number 4 to read the normal body temperature in degrees Celsius.

Exercise f

Answer the following questions. You need to think!

1. Mary said, "I'm very hot! My temperature is _____."
   a. 40°C
   b. 40°F
2. In the winter, it is very cold in North Dakota. The temperature is often below _____.
   a. 32°F
   b. 32°C
3. 100°C is the same as _____°F.
4. A nice temperature for a room is _____.
   a. 70°F
   b. 70°C
5. Susan's baby is sick. The baby's temperature is _____.
   a. 36°C
   b. 98°F
   c. 102°F
6. Are these temperatures the same (S) or different (D)?

   a. 212°F   100°C   _____
   b.   0°F   0°C   _____
   c. 36°F   36°C   _____
   d. −5°F   0°C   _____
   e. 32°F   −5°C   _____

7. Circle the colder temperature.
   a. 212°F   200°C
   b. 98°F   30°C
   c.   0°F   0°C
   d. 32°F   32°C
   e. −5°F   −5°C

8. Mrs. Brown's son is very ill. He has a temperature of 40°C. She wants to call the doctor, but she needs to know her son's temperature in degrees Fahrenheit. Can you help her? These formulas will help you.

$$F = 1.8C + 32 \qquad C = \frac{F - 32}{1.8}$$

OTHER MEASUREMENTS

Temperatures aren't the only systems that are different in the U.S. We also use a different system of measurements. Following you will see a table of metric measurements and U.S. measurements. Length measures how long an object is. Weight measures how heavy an object is. Volume measures the amount that can be put in a container, such as a box or a jar.

American Measurements	Metric Measurements
Length	
12 inches (in.) = 1 foot (ft.)	100 centimeters (cm.) = 1 meter (m.)
3 ft. = 1 yard (yd.)	1000 meters = 1 kilometer (km.)
5,280 ft. = 1 mile (mi.)	
Weight	
16 ounces (oz.) = 1 pound (lb.)	1000 grams (gr.) = 1 kilogram (kg.)
1 U.S. ton = 2,000 lbs.	1 metric ton (m. ton) = 1,000 kgs.
Volume	
1 pint (pt.) = 2 cups (c.)	100 milliliters (ml.) = 1 liter (l)
1 quart (qt.) = 2 pts.	
1 gallon (gal.) = 4 qts.	

Conversions

Length

in. × 2.5 = cm.
ft. × 30 = cm.
yd. × 0.9 = m.
mi. × 1.6 = km.

cm. × 0.4 = in.
m. × 3.3 = ft.
m. × 1.1 = yd.
km. × 0.6 = mi.

Weight

lb. × .45 = kg.
U.S. ton × .907 = m. ton

kg. × 2.2 = lbs.
m. ton × 1.1 = U.S. ton

Volume

pt. × .47 = 1.
qt. × .95 = 1.
gal. × 3.78 = 1.

1. × .525 = pt.
1. × 1.05 = qt.
1. × .262 = gal.

Temperature

$F = 1.8\ C + 32$

$C = \dfrac{F - 32}{1.8}$

Exercise g

Using the conversion table above, answer these questions.

1. In Venezuela, gasoline costs 10 cents per liter. In the U.S., it costs $1.20 per gallon.
   a. Where is gasoline more expensive?
   b. John's car needs 15 gallons of gas. How many liters of gas does he need?
2. Mary has a bad headache. Her temperature is 100°F. Should she call the doctor or take an aspirin and go to bed?
3. You want to go to a warm place for your vacation. You look in the newspaper and see:
   Tampa, Florida   68°F
   Puerto Vallarta, Mexico   25°C
   Where will you go? Why?
4. Steak costs $2.25 a pound. Juanita wants 2 kilos. How much will the steak cost her?
5. Tomatoes in Colorado cost $.69 a pound. Tomatoes in Saudi Arabia cost $.70 a kilo. Where are tomatoes more expensive?

6. Mahmoud is 1.75 meters tall and weighs 80 kilograms. He needs to know his height in feet and his weight in pounds for his U.S. identification card. Can you help him?
7. Jorge is planning a big party for his friends. He bought six quarts of whiskey. His friends gave him four more pints. How many gallons of whiskey does he have? How many liters of whiskey does he have?
8. Mark has $4.00 and he wants to buy some wine. California wine costs eight dollars a gallon. French wine costs sixteen dollars for four liters.

   How much California wine can he buy? _____

   How much French wine can he buy? _____
9. Yoshi and Kumiko drove one hundred miles to visit Yoshi's mother. They drove another three hundred kilometers to visit Kumiko's father. How far did they travel? _____ miles

   _____ kilometers
10. Yoshi and Kumiko's car gets 28 miles to the gallon. Gas costs $1.25 a gallon. How much did they spend on their trip to visit their parents?

   _____

11. American fishermen caught a two-ton whale. Japanese fishermen caught a two-ton whale. Which whale was bigger? How do you know?
12. Mike is 6 feet tall and weighs 180 pounds. Suleiman's height is 1.9 meters and his weight is 67.5 kilograms. Who is taller? _____

   Who is heavier? _____

Exercise h

Read the following passage and answer the questions.

There are many kinds of animals in the world. Some are mammals. Others are reptiles. Still others are insects.

There are many kinds of mammals. Some mammals, like the lion and the giraffe, live in places where the temperature is about 38°C. Others, such as the polar bears and the seals, live in places where the temperature is about 5°C. Still others, for example the whale, live in water where the temperature is about 10°C.

Reptiles like the python and puff adder live in the jungle. The temperature is about 40°C there. Other reptiles, like lizards and rattlesnakes, live in the Rocky Mountains of Colorado. The temperature is about 30°C in the summer and 0°C in the winter. Reptiles dislike cold weather, so when it is very cold, they sleep.

Insects live everywhere. Some live in the air, such as the mosquito and the fly. Others live on land, like the ant. Still others live in the water.

1. How many paragraphs are there in this passage?
   a. 3   c. 1
   b. 4   d. 2
2. Underline the main idea in the second paragraph.
3. Which mammals live in very hot places?
   a. seals and lions   c. giraffes and lions
   b. giraffes and whales   d. whales and polar bears
4. Which mammals live in very cold places?
   a. polar bears and giraffes   c. seals and lions
   b. whales and lions   d. polar bears and seals

5. Rattlesnakes sleep in the winter because _____.
   a. the temperature is 30°C   c. they like very cold
   b. they don't like cold   temperatures
      temperatures   d. they are very tired
6. Circle the word in paragraph 3 that has a prefix.
7. Underline the main idea of the fourth paragraph.
8. How many examples of insects are in paragraph 4?
   a. 3   c. 1
   b. 2   d. 4
9. Whales live in water where the temperature is about
   a. 38°C   c. 98°F
   b. 10°F   d. 50°F
10. Pythons and puff adders live in places where the temperature is
    about _____.
    a. 40°F   c. 30°F
    b. 104°F   d. 0°F
11. A good title for this passage is
    a. Animals   c. Animals and Temperatures
    b. Temperatures   d. Mammals and Reptiles

12. What do these words mean?
   a. there (paragraph 3 line 2)
   b. they (paragraph 3 line 5)

Exercise i

Follow the directions carefully using your own piece of paper.

1. Write your name (last name first) in the upper left-hand corner.
2. Make a circle under your name.
3. Write the normal body temperature (°C) inside the circle.
4. Write the date today in the upper right-hand corner.
5. Write the names of three mammals in the lower right-hand corner.
6. Alphabetize the names of the mammals.
7. Make a rectangle in the lower left-hand corner.
8. Write a word beginning with *re-* inside the rectangle.

Reference Books

Exercise a
Read this paragraph and answer the questions.

Reference books are very useful for students. Students refer to, look at, these books when they need information about a specific topic, subject. The general reference books are dictionaries, encyclopedias, and atlases (maps). There are also special reference books for specific fields, such as a dictionary of business and finance, an encyclopedia of music, etc. Reference books are in libraries. Usually people cannot take these books out of the library. They use them in the library, or they copy the information they need.

1. The author explains the following words. What do they mean?
   a. refer to
   b. topic
   c. atlas
2. What do the pronouns refer to?
   a. they (line 2)
   b. They (line 7)
   c. them (line 7)

3. Circle the examples you see in this paragraph.

4. Which reference book(s) does the student need?

   a. Juanita needs to know the capital city of South Dakota.

   b. Fatima needs to know the meaning of a word.

   c. Kumiko wants to know about reptiles.

Exercise b

Read the passage and answer the questions.

DICTIONARIES

Dictionaries contain a lot of information, so they are a very useful reference book. Some of the information is very important for foreign students. Some of the information is less important, but it is interesting.

The most useful information in the dictionary for foreign students is the spelling, meaning, synonyms, and antonyms of words. The dictionary shows how to spell (write correctly) the words including irregular verbs and plurals. Because most words have more than one meaning, it is important to choose the correct meaning for the word you want. To help you choose the correct meaning, the dictionary shows the parts of speech, such as noun, verb, adjective, etc. for each meaning, definition. In addition, the dictionary shows if the word is formal or slang (usually used only in speaking but not in writing). Finally, the dictionary gives synonyms, words with almost the same meaning, and antonyms, words with the opposite meaning. All of this information is very helpful for foreign students.

The dictionary contains additional information. It tells how to pronounce the word, tells how to divide the word into syllables, and gives the history of the word, that is, if the word came from Latin, German, etc. The dictionary also contains general information about people and places. It often gives the population and location of cities and countries and tells when famous people, like Cleopatra, lived.

1. The writer explains these words. What do they mean?

   a. spell

   b. definition

    c. slang

    d. synonym

    e. antonym

2. What do these pronouns refer to?

    a. they (paragraph 1 line 1)

    b. it (paragraph 1 line 3)

    c. It (paragraph 3 line 1)

    d. It (paragraph 3 line 5)

3. Circle the examples in the passage.

4. According to the passage, are the following interesting or important for foreign students?

    a. _____ meaning

    b. _____ synonym

    c. _____ when people lived

    d. _____ antonym

    e. _____ pronunciation

    f. _____ number of syllables

    g. _____ spelling

    h. _____ history of the word

GUIDE WORDS

At the top of each page in a dictionary are two words. They are called guide words. The guide words tell the first word on the page of the dictionary and the last word on the page. Look at these pages from a dictionary.

cat	100	cemetery	cent	101	chance
cat		catch	cent		Chad
catalog		cattle	century		chain
ca ...		cave	ce ...		cha ...
ca ...		celebrate	certain		cha ...
ca ...		Celsius	cer ...		chalk
ca ...		cemetery	cer ...		chance

What are the guide words on page 100? _____

What is the first word on page 100? _____

What is the last word on page 100? _____

The other words on page 100 come between the words *cat* and *cemetery* alphabetically.

Exercise c

Write these words in alphabetical order.

cat	catch	chance
cash	carry	center
catalog	Celsius	cemetery
cattle	Centigrade	cent
		change

1. _____

2. _____

3. _____

4. _____

5. _____

6. _____

7. _____

8. _____

9. _____

10. _____

11. _____

12. _____

13. _____

Exercise d

On the alphabetized list above, circle the guide words you saw on page 100. Make a rectangle around the guide words you saw on page 101.

Look at the word *carry*. It is before the word *cat*. The word *carry* is not on page 100. It is probably on page 98 or 99.

Look at the word *catch*. It is after the word *cat*, and it is before the word *cemetery*. Therefore, the word *catch* is on page 100.

Look at the word *Centigrade*. It is after the word *cent*, and it is before the word *chance*. Therefore, it is on page 101.

Which of the above words are on page 100?

Which of the above words are on page 101?

What page are these words on?
  change
  cash

We also find guide words in encyclopedias and telephone books. The guide words help us find the information (word or name) quickly.

Exercise e

Look at the following guide words and answer the question.

Page 15   cab   – car
Page 16   cart   – cat
Page 17   ceiling – corn
Page 18   cost   – cute

On what page could you find these words?

1. cabinet
2. coin
3. come
4. call
5. cold
6. cut
7. can
8. candy
9. castle
10. couch

Exercise f

Look at the following guide words and answer the question.

Page 115   game – gaze
Page 116   gel   – giraffe
Page 117   give – golf
Page 118   gone – gun

On what page could you find these words?

1. goal
2. gate
3. gum
4. gentleman
5. god
6. gasoline
7. garage
8. germ
9. gold
10. glove
11. gorilla
12. gin

Exercise g

Look at the following guide words and answer the question.

Page 9   a   – addict
Page 10   address – apple
Page 11   approach – around
Page 12   arrest   – attack
Page 13   aunt   – auxiliary
Page 14   avenue   – baby

On what page could you find these words?

1. appendix
2. apricot
3. ask
4. average
5. acid

6. aster

7. Arabic

8. aluminum

9. answer

10. apron

11. automatic

12. arson

13. after

14. Austria

15. across

16. approximate

17. away

18. about

MEANINGS

After you find the word in the dictionary, you need to choose the correct meaning. Many words in English have more than one meaning. You find the correct meaning by looking at the grammar, noun, verb, etc., and the other words in the sentence. Look at the following words.

bridge:	1.	*noun*	a card game
	2.	*noun*	a structure that takes a road over a river
	3.	*noun*	the part of the nose between the eyes
fork:	1.	*noun*	a pronged instrument used for eating
	2.	*noun*	the place where a long narrow object, such as a river or road, divides
light:	1.	*adj.*	not heavy
	2.	*adj.*	not dark
	3.	*noun*	lamp, especially electric
lot:	1.	*noun*	a large amount
	2.	*noun*	an area of land used for parking or building
right:	1.	*adj.*	correct; opposite of wrong
	2.	*adj.*	direction; opposite of left

Exercise h

Read the following sentences and decide which definition is correct for the italicized word in each sentence.

1. They built the *bridge* just before the *fork* in the river.
2. I can't see. Would you please turn on the *light*?
3. He knows a *lot* of English now.
4. Do I turn *right* at the traffic light?
5. They drove over the *bridge.*
6. I like the *light* blue shirt more than the dark blue one.
7. After dinner, they played *bridge.*
8. She took the *forks* out of the dishwasher.
9. You must pay $4.00 if you put your car in this *lot.*
10. People need heavy coats in the winter, but in the spring they need only *light* coats.
11. The *bridge* of my eyeglasses broke. I need to have it repaired.
12. I think you're *right* and the teacher is wrong.

Exercise i

Read the passage and answer the questions.

ENCYCLOPEDIAS

Another useful reference book is the encyclopedia. An encyclopedia is a group of volumes (books) that contain short articles about specific topics. The articles are arranged alphabetically and give more specific information about a subject than a dictionary does. For example, if you look for the word *bird* in the dictionary, you will probably find a two- or three-sentence explanation. In the encyclopedia, you will probably find a two or three-page explanation with illustrations. Encyclopedias also use guide words so that you can find the information you want very quickly. In an encyclopedia, you can find articles about famous people, places, foods, animals, etc. There are also encyclopedias for specific fields, such as music, engineering, technology, and religion. Most students have their own dictionaries; however, they usually go to a library when they want to use the encyclopedia.

1. What are volumes?
2. Underline the examples you see in this paragraph.
3. How is an encyclopedia similar to a dictionary?
4. How is an encyclopedia different from a dictionary?

Exercise j

Look at this set of encyclopedias (figure 39). Use these volumes to answer the questions.

figure 39

A	B	CD	EF	G	HI	JK	L	M	N	OP	QR	S	TU	VW	XYZ
1	2	3	4	5	6	7	8	9	10	11	12	13	14	15	16

1. There are _____ volumes in this set of encyclopedias.

2. Information about thermometers is in Volume _____.

3. A picture of a heart is in Volume _____.

4. Which are in the same volume?

    a. apes and elephants   c. fish and flies

    b. eggs and cheese   d. horses and monkeys

5. Four things in Volume 9 are _____, _____,

    _____, and _____.

Exercise k

Look at this set of encyclopedias. (figure 40). Use these volumes to answer the questions.

figure 40

A	BC	DEF	G	HIJ	KL	M	N	O	PQ	R	S	T	UVW	XYZ
1	2	3	4	5	6	7	8	9	10	11	12	13	14	15

1. There are _____ volumes in this set of encyclopedias.

2. You want to know more about reptiles. You need Volume _____.

3. Information about butterflies is in Volume _____.

4. Which are in the same volume?
   a. cat and dog
   b. fish and gorilla
   c. snake and turtle
   d. dog and elephant

5. Name two things you can find in Volume 13.

6. Name four things that are in Volume 3.

Exercise l

Look at this set of encyclopedias (figure 41). Use these volumes to answer the questions.

figure 41

AB	C	D	EF	GH	IJK	LM	NOP	QR	STU	VWX	YZ
1	2	3	4	5	6	7	8	9	10	11	12

1. There are _____ volumes in this set of encyclopedias.

2. You want to know more about Ghana. You need Volume _____.

3. Information about whales is in Volume _____.

4. Which are in the same volume?
   a. eggs and bacon
   b. ice cream and jungle
   c. potatoes and rabbits
   d. Nebraska and Ohio

5. Name two things that are in Volume 2.

6. Name three things that are in Volume 11.

Exercise m

Sometimes the volumes of an encyclopedia are arranged differently. Look at this set of encyclopedias (figure 42) and answer the questions.

A-ARGOL	ARGON- BEDS	BEDW- BRON	BRONZ- CELL	CELLI- COMIC	COMIN- DEAFM	DEAFN- EDUC	EDUD- EXPL
1	2	3	4	5	6	7	8
FAB- FOX	FRAN- GILA	GILB- HANS	HANU- IDAG	IDAH- JEW	JEWE- LEUH	LEUK- MENC	MEND- NEGRA
9	10	11	12	13	14	15	16
NEGRE- PAN	PAP- POTA	POTE- RAVE	RAVI- SCHOO	SCHOU- SPAI	SPE- TECA	TECH- ULTA	ULTE- WASE
17	18	19	20	21	22	23	24
WASH- Z							
25							

figure 42

1. There are _____ volumes in this encyclopedia.
2. Name two things in Volume 12.
3. Information about mammals is in Volume _____.
4. Information about calendars is in Volume _____.
5. Information about insects is in Volume _____.
6. Information about vegetables is in Volume _____.
7. Information about fruit is in Volume _____.
8. Which are in the same volume?
   a. ear and elbow   c. Celsius and Centigrade
   b. reptiles and snakes   d. hair and head

10

Taking Tests

Exercise a

Preview the passage on the following pages. Then answer the questions.

Title: _____

Subtitles: _____

_____

1. What two types of tests will you read about?
2. Are there example questions in this passage? How do you know?

TAKING TESTS

There are two basic types of tests, exams, that are used in American schools and universities. They are the objective test and the subjective test. The objective test provides, gives, all the information you need to answer a question. A subjective exam asks you to give your own idea about the answer.

Objective Exams. There are several common kinds of objective exams. The most common types contain the TRUE–FALSE question and the multiple-choice question. Other question types include matching and sentence completion.

The most important part of taking an objective exam is reading *carefully*. You need to read the instructions very carefully, and you need to read each question carefully.

In a TRUE–FALSE question, the teacher or professor is asking you to say if a sentence is correct (TRUE) or incorrect (FALSE). The instructions are not always the same for these questions, so you need to read them carefully. For example:

Directions: Read the following sentences. If they are true, write t. If they are false, write f.

    _____ 1. Many foreign students must take the TOEFL exam before they begin their university classes.

Directions: Read the following sentences. If they are true, write t. If they are false, write f *and* correct the sentence to make it true.

    _____ 2. All foreign students study English before they begin their university classes.

    _____ 3. Most foreign students study English before they begin their university classes.

Important words in TRUE–FALSE questions include *all, always, everyone, everything, no, never,* and *no one.* These words usually make a sentence false. The "correct" or "true" sentences often include the words *many, most, few, a little,* and *some.*

Multiple-choice questions ask you to choose the best answer from a group of answers (usually four). Again, there are small variations, differences, in the directions, so you need to read them carefully. For example:

Directions: Choose the answer that best completes the sentence. Blacken the letter of the answer on your answer sheet (figure 43).

    1. Another word that means variations is
        a. answers
        b. differences
        c. directions
        d. choices

	A	B	C	D
1	○	○	○	○
2	○	○	○	○
3	○	○	○	○

figure 43

Directions: Circle the letter of the response that best answers the question.

    2. How many basic kinds of exams are there?
        a. 2
        b. 1
        c. 4
        d. 8

Directions: Choose the answer that best completes the sentence. Write the letter of the answer in the space provided.

_____ 3. An objective exam
        a. gives you the answer
        b. asks you to select the best answer
        c. requires a lot of reading
        d. all of the above

The instructions for multiple-choice questions usually ask you to select the *best* answer, not a *correct* answer. Reading each possible answer is important because you will often see possible answers, like

both a and b
none of the above
all of the above

Matching questions ask you to match one (find the similar) answer with another. For example:

Directions: Match the following words with their meanings. Write the letter of the correct response in the space provided.

_____ 1. rewrite   a. to look at again

_____ 2. review   b. person who writes

_____ 3. unreadable   c. write again

                              d. person who doesn't read

                              e. something we can't read

Sentence completion items ask you to finish a sentence or give a list from the information you have learned, remembered. For example:

Directions: Complete the following.

1. Animals that live both on land and in the water include

   _____, _____, and _____.

2. Three characteristics of mammals are _____,

   _____ and _____.

In completion questions, there are often many possible correct answers. You may choose any of them to complete the question correctly. It is not necessary to use complete sentences; a one-word answer or a phrase (a few words) is all that is necessary.

Subjective Exams. The second type of exam is called a subjective exam because the student can use his or her own ideas to answer the question. The student can organize the information in any way he or she wishes. Teachers look for the information, the explanation, and the organization when they correct the test.

There are two major kinds of subjective questions: essay and short answer. Essay questions require, need, a much longer answer, usually from several paragraphs to several pages. Short-answer questions usually require a shorter answer, such as several sentences or a paragraph.

In a subjective test, the amount of time you are given will tell you how long your answer should be. If you have two questions to answer in an hour, you will probably spend thirty minutes on each question. If you have only one question, your answer will be much longer.

Before beginning to answer a subjective question, it is a good idea to spend a few minutes thinking about what information you want to include and how to organize this information. It is very important to read the question carefully. There are several key, important, words that are frequently, often, used. They are:

COMPARE AND CONTRAST: This means show how several things are similar (compare) or different (contrast) or both.

DISCUSS: This means explain the problem and/or talk about both sides of any argument or question.

ENUMERATE: This means list your ideas as briefly, shortly, as possible. Do not include any examples or details.

ILLUSTRATE: This means show by example, diagram, or figure.

SUMMARIZE: This means give only the main ideas of an individual or a theory.

DEFINE: This means give the general category *and* the specific distinguishing features.

Sometimes, two of these words may be included in one longer question. For example: Summarize the roles of the three branches of the U.S. federal government and illustrate how they work together.

In a subjective test, your English and your organization can be as important as the information you include in your answer.

It is very useful to know what kind of exam your teacher has pre-pared when you are studying for a test. If you know the kind of test, you can imagine, guess, the kinds of questions the teacher might write. You then know what to study very carefully, and what to review less completely.

Exercise b

Complete this outline for the passage *Taking Tests*.

I. Objective exams
   A. Most important
      1. Read _____ carefully
      2. Read _____ carefully
   B. Kinds of questions
      1. True–False
         a. Words used in a false sentence: _____
         b. Words used in a true sentence: _____
      2. Multiple choice
      3. _____
      4. _____

II. _____ exams
   A. Important
      1. _____
      2. _____
   B. Kinds of _____
      1. Essay
         a. Length: _____
      2. _____
         a. Length: _____
   C. Frequently used words
      1. _____ =
      2. _____ =
      3. _____ =

4. _____ =

5. _____ =

6. _____ =

Exercise c

Study the passage *Taking Tests*. Then answer these questions without looking back at the passage. You have 50 minutes to answer all the questions.

I.   Are the following statements true or false? Circle T or F and correct the false statements to make them true.

T   F   1. An objective exam is always easier than a subjective exam.

T   F   2. You usually write more on a subjective exam than on an objective exam.

T   F   3. Spelling is never important on an objective exam.

T   F   4. An objective exam is easier for the professors to correct, grade.

II.   Circle the letter of the best answer.

5. Which of the following is *not* a kind of objective exam?
   a. essay
   b. true–false
   c. multiple choice
   d. matching

6. Which of the following words often make a statement true?
   a. always
   b. often
   c. never
   d. all of the above

7. The most important part of taking an objective exam is
   a. reading quickly
   b. writing quickly
   c. reading carefully
   d. writing long answers

8. Two important parts of a subjective exam are
   a. reading and writing
   b. organizing and explaining
   c. writing and rereading
   d. reading and organizing

III. Write short answers for the following.
   1. What are three important words in an essay exam?

   2. Objective   questions   include   _____,
      _____, and _____.

   3. Why is reading very important in an objective exam?

4. How do you know how much to write in an essay exam?

IV. Answer any *two* of the following essay questions.

    1. Define the following: objective exam and subjective exam.

    2. Compare and contrast objective and subjective exams.

    3. In your opinion, which kind of exam is easier? Discuss.

Exercise d

Read the following paragraphs. Practice writing questions for each paragraph, both objective and subjective. Exchange books with a classmate and answer the questions.

Paragraph 1

Scientists can classify the million different kinds of animals that live in the world. They give names to groups of animals. Scientists call these groups "classes." The animals in each class are alike, the same, in some ways, and they are unlike all the other groups in some ways. Some examples of the classes are the insect class, the bird class, and the mammal class. An ant is a kind of insect, so it is like other insects and unlike birds. An owl is a bird and different from mammals. An example from the mammal class is a tiger. All mammals have hair, and all birds have feathers.

Paragraph 2

The zebra is an interesting member of the horse family. A zebra is between four and five feet high. It is a horse with a strong body and a heavy head. Zebras live in open, grassy areas of Africa. These animals move together in large groups with other animals, like antelopes. All of these animals can run fast to escape their enemies. Zebras also have stripes, black and white lines, on their bodies for protection. These stripes protect the zebra from enemies, such as the lion and the tiger, because these wild cats can't see the striped horse in the tall grass.

Paragraph 3

Court games, games played on a court, are popular in some countries, such as the U.S., where the winter is long and cold. These games are popular because they can be played indoors. They require a limited amount of space, so the court can be inside a building.

Tennis, an especially popular court game, can be played indoors or outdoors. However, tennis players like the indoor courts in the winter. This is also true for similar court games, like badminton, handball, and raquetball. Although there are courts for these games outside, the indoor courts get more use during the cold weather.

The most popular game that is played on an indoor court is basketball. Basketball is a team sport, like football or soccer. In basketball, one team competes with another team to score more points. A player makes points by passing a ball through a basket at the opposing team's end of the court. The basket is a ring of steel, a strong metal, that hangs higher than the players' heads. Each time a player makes a pass through the metal ring, a basket, his team gets one or two points.

Paragraph 4

The federal government of the United States has three branches: the legislative, the executive, and the judicial. The legislative branch makes the laws. The executive branch carries out the laws. The judicial branch interprets the laws. The President heads the executive branch. The Supreme Court heads the judicial branch. The legislative branch includes both houses of Congress: the Senate and the House of Representatives. The Constitution limits the powers of each branch and pre-vents one branch from gaining too much power. This system has worked for over two hundred years.

11

Computers

THIS/THESE

Writers often use two important words: *this* and *these*. Both words are a way of repeating a word or an idea. *This* is a singular word. *These* is a plural word. When you see these words, you need to look in the sentence before. Look at the following paragraph.

Americans love pets. (These animals) are a part of their families. People who live in apartments often have a cat or a small dog because (these animals) don't require, need, a lot of space. People who have a large yard often have a large dog. (This pet) needs to spend a lot of time running outside. There are pets for all kinds of families.

Exercise a

Read the following paragraphs. Look for the words *this* and *these*. Then answer the questions.

Computers are becoming more and more popular. Many small businesses such as shoe stores and restaurants are using small office computers. These businesses use computers for jobs, such as keeping inventory (counting how many shoes they have sold, and counting how many and what kinds they still have.) These computers can help the business-person make decisions about what to order, buy, etc.

1. Circle the examples in this paragraph.
2. Underline the main idea in the paragraph.
3. What does inventory mean?
4. What do the following refer to?
   a. These businesses
   b. These computers

Home computers are also very popular. Everyone in the family can use these small, inexpensive devices. Children enjoy playing video games, like Pac-Man and River Raiders, on them. In addition, they can use these aids to learn and review schoolwork. Adults often use these computers to help with the household budget, amount of money to spend. These versatile machines can also type letters.

1. Underline the main idea of this paragraph.
2. What does budget mean?
3. Circle the examples in this paragraph.
4. What do the following refer to?
   a. these devices
   b. these aids
   c. these computers
   d. these versatile machines

Exercise b

As you are reading the passage, *Computers*, look for the answer to the following questions.

1. What are computers?
2. Are all computers large?
3. Name three things a computer can do.
4. What are the two main kinds of computers?
5. Where are analog computers often used? Why?
6. How many parts does a digital computer have?
7. Why does a computer need a program?
8. Where do we see computers?

COMPUTERS

Computers are machines that help people find answers to their questions. There are many kinds of computers. Some are very large; others are so small that we can put them in our pockets. The two basic, main, kinds of computers are analog and digital.

Computers can do many things. They can solve, answer, mathematics problems, record airline reservations, help in space flights and direct nuclear weapons. They can even speak and make translations from one language to another.

Analog computers measure physical quantities, such as the movement of electricity or temperatures. This kind of computer, however, often does only *one* job. For example, it guides, directs, planes. Analog computers are often used in factories to control machines, to aim guns, and to help ships and planes stay on course (in the correct direction).

Digital computers count numbers. These devices are very adaptable, so they are more popular than analog computers. Digital computers are often programmed, (instructed) to work alone, without people. This device can make choices in the middle of a problem. For example, if in the middle of a problem, the computer sees a positive number, it will continue working on the problem. If it sees a negative number, it will stop working.

Every digital computer has five basic parts: the input, the memory, the control, the logic, and the output. The input is the information we put in the computer, like the data, numbers, and the instructions. The memory holds this information until it is needed for the problem. The control device decides where and when to send the information. The logic section solves the problem by using the instructions. The output section puts the information out. Sometimes it is on paper. Sometimes it is on a TV screen.

A computer needs to have a program in order to work. A computer program is the group, set, of directions that a computer needs to solve a problem. Programmers are the people who write these instructions in a computer language, such as COBOL for business or FORTRAN for math and science. These instructions include a code which tells the computer what to do and an address which tells it where to find the necessary information in its memory.

We see computers almost everywhere around us. They are in businesses, stores, airports, schools, and homes. The young children learn to use them in their classes. Some people are unhappy about the computer revolution, but it is here to stay.

Exercise c

Answer the following questions.

1. The author explains the following words. What do they mean?
   a. basic
   b. solve
   c. guides
   d. on course
   e. alone
   g. data
   h. programmer

2. What do the following pronouns refer to?
   a. them, (paragraph 1 line 3)
   b. They, (paragraph 2 line 3)
   c. it, (paragraph 3 line 3)
   d. they, (paragraph 4 line 2)
   e. it, (paragraph 4 line 5)
   f. it, (paragraph 5 line 4)
   g. it (paragraph 5 line 7)
   h. it (paragraph 6 line 6)
   i. them (paragraph 7 line 3)
   j. it (paragraph 7 line 4)

3. What do the following refer to?
   a. This kind of computer, (paragraph 3 line 2)
   b. These devices, (paragraph 4 line 1)
   c. This device, (paragraph 4 line 3-4)
   d. this information, (paragraph 5 line 4)
   e. These instructions, (paragraph 6 line 5)

4. Circle the examples in this passage.

5. Underline the main idea in each paragraph.

Exercise d

From the information in paragraph 5, label this diagram (figure 44).

TITLE _____

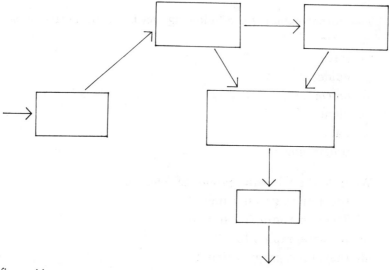

figure 44

Exercise e

Complete this outline for the passage, *Computers*.

    I. Computers = _____
      A. Analog

        1. Measure _____

          a. Examples: _____ and _____
        2. Can do only _____ job.
        3. Uses

          a. _____

          b. _____

          c. _____

      B. _____

        1. Count _____

        2. Works without _____

3. _____ basic parts

    a. _____

    b. _____

    c. _____

    d. _____

    e. _____

C. Programs = _____

  1. Programmer = _____

  2. Languages

    a. _____

    b. _____

  3. Include _____ and _____

Exercise f

From the information on this outline, write five objective questions on a separate paper. Exchange questions with a classmate. Can you answer the questions without looking at your outline?

Exercise g

Read this passage and answer the questions.

HISTORY OF COMPUTERS

The beginning of computers began hundreds and hundreds of years ago. In the seventeenth century, the first calculators, machines that can solve mathematics problems, were made. In 1644 Blaise Pascal made a machine that could add (+) and subtract (−). In 1673 Gottfried Liebnitz made a calculator that could also multiply (×) and divide (÷). In the 1870's, Lord Kelvin built the first computer. He used this device to predict ocean tides.

In the twentieth century, we have seen many, many improvements. In the 1930's, Dr. Vannevar Bush at the Massachusetts Institute of Technology, MIT, built the first modern computer. It was very, very big. In 1943, scientists at Harvard built the Mark I. In 1946,

ENIAC, Electronic Numerical Integrator and Computer, was built at the University of Pennsylvania. ENIAC was the first electronic computer. It weighed sixty-thousand pounds and used vacuum tubes. In 1959, transistors were developed. These devices allowed people to build powerful computers that were very, very small and much less expensive. Today, computers are becoming more and more powerful, and smaller and smaller.

1. What do the following mean?
   a. calculators
   b. MIT
   c. +
   d. −
   e. ×
   f. ÷
   g. ENIAC

2. What do the following refer to?
   a. He (paragraph 1 line 6)
   b. this device (paragraph 1 line 6)
   c. It (paragraph 2 line 3)
   d. It (paragraph 2 line 7)
   e. These devices (paragraph 2 line 8)

3. How many kilograms did the ENIAC weigh?

4. What happened in the 17th century?

5. What happened in the 19th century?

6. What happened in the 20th century?

7. In the list below, what happened first, second, etc?

   _____ A small, inexpensive computer was built.

   _____ Mark I was built.

   _____ A calculator that could add and subtract was built.

   _____ ENIAC was built.

   _____ Transistors were developed.

   _____ The first modern computer was built.

   _____ A calculator that could add, subtract, multiply, and divide was built.

Exercise h

Read this passage and answer the questions.

HOW TO SELECT (CHOOSE) A HOME COMPUTER

Because computers are versatile (can do many things), such as teach, play games, or help with a business, choosing a computer is not a simple, easy, job. If you follow these steps, you will find this task easier.

First, decide on the main reason(s) that you want a computer. Is the most important reason to play games or to help with your business or to help with schoolwork?

Second, look carefully at the programs the computer can use. Are there enough available for your needs? Some people also write their own programs. If you want to write your own, it's important to consider, look at, the computer language. Is it easy to learn?

Third, decide on the minimum, the least, smallest, needs you have for your computer. What are the characteristics you would like to have? For example, do you want a typewriter keyboard? Is a color display important to you? Your use of the computer will help you decide which characteristics are necessary, which are desirable (nice), and which are unnecessary.

Fourth, when you have limited your choices to a few computers, look at the secondary uses and programs. For example, if your main reason for buying a home computer is to play games, you may decide to take Computer A instead of Computer B because Computer A also can be used as a word processor.

Fifth, consider the cost. There are two costs to think about. The first cost is the price you must pay to take the computer home. The second is the price of additional programs and possible additions that you might want to buy at a later date.

Be sure to try out the computer before you buy it. Salespeople at computer stores are happy to help you choose the computer that will best fit your needs and budget.

1. What do the following words mean?
   a. select
   b. simple
   c. consider

d. task
e. minimum
f. desirable
g. versatile

2. Name three reasons someone might want a home computer.

3. What kinds of programs would the people in question 2 need? (Guess!)

4. What are four specific characteristics a person might need in a computer?

5. What are the two costs to consider?

6. Why is it a good idea to try out a computer before you buy it?

7. Why is choosing a computer difficult?

8. Underline the words in the passage that have prefixes and suffixes.

Exercise i

Read this passage and answer the questions.

COMPUTERS IN THE SUPERMARKET

Computers are now very common in supermarkets. They use the UPC. UPC means Universal Product Code. This code is now on most cans and boxes of food. The lines and numbers of the code do not tell the price. Instead, they tell the computer exactly what the product is. The computer reads the code and knows the price. It can then add up the bill very quickly. Because this machine works so quickly, people, shoppers, spend less time waiting in lines. Also, prices may be lower because supermarkets no longer have to hire people (give people the job) to put the prices on each can and box. Still another benefit, good thing, is that computers never make a mistake, but people sometimes do. So, for supermarkets, the computer and the UPC systems are very helpful.

1. What do the following words mean?
   a. UPC
   b. shoppers
   c. hire
   d. benefit

2. What do the following refer to?
   a. They (line 1)
   b. This code (line 2)
   c. they (line 4)
   d. It (line 5)
   e. this machine (line 6)

3. The code is
   a. prices
   b. lines
   c. numbers
   d. both b and c

4. The machine knows what the product is because of
   a. the shoppers
   b. the lines and numbers
   c. the people working at the store
   d. both b and c

5. Tell three ways computers help supermarkets.

6. Circle the words with affixes.
7. Underline the main idea in the paragraph.

12

The American Government

Exercise a

Preview the passage, *The Federal Government of the United States.*

Title: _____

Subtitles: _____

_____

_____

_____

_____

_____

Exercise b

Answer these questions from the information above.

1. What is the subject of this passage?
2. How many parts are there in the U.S. federal government?
3. What are the three parts of the government?

Exercise c

Number the paragraphs in the passage.

Look at this chart (figure 45). In which paragraph(s) could you find the information?

	LEGISLATIVE	EXECUTIVE	JUDICIAL
Membership	para._____	para._____	para._____
Job	para._____	para._____	para._____

figure 45

Exercise d

The author explains the following words. Look for them while you are reading.

1. federal
2. branches
3. elected
4. laws
5. members
6. population
7. senators
8. approves
9. treaties
10. accepts
11. examines
12. resigned
13. cabinet
14. serve
15. secretary
16. enforced

17. Armed Forces
18. appointed
19. kidnapping
20. counterfeiting
21. justices
22. interpret
23. powerful
24. sign
25. checks and balances

THE FEDERAL GOVERNMENT
OF THE UNITED STATES

The federal, central, government of the United States has three branches, parts. They are the legislative branch, the executive branch, and the judicial branch. Each branch has special jobs, but they work together to provide a central government for the U.S.

The Legislative Branch. The legislative branch is often called the Congress. It has two parts: the House of Representatives and the Senate. The Congress meets in the Capitol Building in Washington, D.C. The members of Congress are elected, chosen, by the American people. The Congress is responsible for making the laws, rules, for the entire country.

The House of Representatives has 435 members, people. It has more members than the Senate because each state sends representatives based on its population (the number of people living in the state). For example, the population of Colorado is 2,889,735, so Colorado sends six representatives to Washington. New York's population is 17,558,072, so it sends thirty-four representatives. These men or women work for two years. A representative must be at least 25 years old and a citizen of the U.S.

The Senate has 100 members who are called senators. Each state has two senators. They are elected by the people in their state for a six-year term. A senator must be at least 30 years old and an American citizen. In addition to making laws, the Senate also approves (agrees on) the President's choice for ambassadors, judges in the Supreme Court, and treaties (agreements) with other countries.

The Role of the Legislative Branch. The senators and representatives discuss new laws. Sometimes the Senate wants a new law but the House of Representatives does not, so there is no new law. When both the Senate and the House of Representatives want a new law, they send it to the President. When the President accepts (says yes to) it, we have a new law. When the President does not accept it, we don't have a new law unless 66 percent of the Congress votes for it again.

The Congress also examines, looks at, the activities of the executive branch. If Congress is unhappy, it tries to change the situation. For example, the Senate and House of Representatives examined the Watergate problem, and finally Richard Nixon resigned, quit, the President's job.

The Executive Branch. The executive branch is made up of the President of the United States, the vice-president, the cabinet (a group of secretaries), and many agencies, like the Post Office.

The President is the head of the federal government. He is elected by the people every four years. A president must be at least 35 years old and an American citizen. He may be reelected once, so he may serve, work, for a maximum of eight years. He works and lives in the White House in Washington, D.C.

The executive branch has thirteen departments. Each department has a secretary, the chief of the department. These thirteen secretaries are the President's cabinet. They give him advice and help to make sure that the laws of the country are carried out.

The Role of the Executive Branch. The executive branch makes sure that the laws made by Congress are enforced, carried out. In addition, the President makes treaties with other countries and chooses ambassadors, judges, and his cabinet members. He is the Supreme (highest) Commander of the Armed Forces: the Army, the Navy, and the Air Force. He receives foreign visitors, like ambassadors and heads of governments. He and his cabinet determine foreign policy. However, most of the decisions made by the executive branch must be approved by the Senate.

The Judicial Branch. The judicial branch is made up of several levels of courts. The lowest court is the District Court. There are District Courts in every state. The next higher court is the Court of Appeal, and finally the highest federal court is the Supreme Court located in

Washington D.C. In addition to these federal courts, there are many state courts.

The federal judges are appointed, chosen, by the President for life. These appointments must be approved by the Senate.

The Role of the Judicial Branch. Federal courts make decisions about federal laws, such as kidnapping (taking someone and asking for money), and counterfeiting (making unofficial money). The state courts decide about problems such as speeding tickets and drinking violations.

The Supreme Court has 9 judges, called justices. They decide if a law from Congress follows the American Constitution or does not. In addition, they interpret, explain, the law. The decision is made by the majority of the nine justices, and their decision is final.

The roles of these three branches of the federal government work together so that no one branch can become too powerful, strong. The Congress must approve the President's choices; the President must sign, agree to, the new laws; the Supreme Court makes sure that the new laws agree with the Constitution. This system is called checks and balances. It has worked well for over two hundred years.

Exercise e

Complete the chart on page 153 with the correct information.

Exercise f

What do the following pronouns refer to?

1. They (paragraph 1 line 2)
2. It (paragraph 3 line 1)
3. its (paragraph 3 line 3)
4. These men or women (paragraph 3 line 6)
5. They (paragraph 4 line 2)
6. they (paragraph 5 line 4)
7. it (paragraph 5 line 5)
8. it (paragraph 5 line 5)
9. it (paragraph 6 line 2)
10. They (paragraph 9 line 3)
11. his (paragraph 10 line 7)
12. They (paragraph 14 line 1)

13. their (paragraph 14 line 4)
14. these three branches (paragraph 15 line 1)
15. This system (paragraph 15 line 5)
16. It (paragraph 15 line 6)

Exercise g

Circle the words with prefixes and suffixes in this passage.

Exercise h

Draw a rectangle around the examples in the passage.

Exercise i

Complete this outline of the passage.

    I. The federal government of the U.S.

        A. Legislative branch = _____

            1. Location: _____

            2. Components (parts)

                a. House of Representatives = _____ members

                    (1) _____

                    (2) _____

                b. Senate = _____ members

                    (1) _____

                    (2) _____

            3. Jobs

                a. _____

                b. _____

                c. _____

        B. Executive branch

            1. Location: _____

            2. Components

                a. _____

                    (1) _____

                    (2) _____

b. Cabinet = _____ members

(1) _____

(2) _____

3. Jobs

a. _____

b. _____

c. _____

C. _____

1. _____

2. _____

a. _____

b. _____

c. _____

3. _____

a. _____

b. _____

Exercise j

Answer these questions by looking at your outline.

1. Which branch of the government makes new laws?
2. Which branch of the government makes treaties with other countries?
3. Which branch of the government decides if the laws follow the Constitution?
4. How many senators does California have?
5. What are the components of the judicial branch?
6. How long does a president work?
7. How many justices are on the Supreme Court?

Exercise k

Are the following statements true, false, or unknown?

1. James Richards is twenty-seven years old. He　　YES　　NO　　?
   can be a representative.

2. Pat Murray became a senator in 1984. She will   YES   NO   ?
   stay in the Senate until 1990.
3. The President and the Senate must agree on   YES   NO   ?
   many things.
4. The President and the Supreme Court must   YES   NO   ?
   agree on many things.
5. Representatives and senators need two homes: YES   NO   ?
   one in Washington D.C. and one in their home
   state.
6. The population of Ohio is larger than the   YES   NO   ?
   population of Wyoming. Ohio sends more
   senators than Wyoming.
7. Justices are usually not young people.   YES   NO   ?

Exercise I

Read this paragraph and answer the questions.

THE AMERICAN JUDICIAL SYSTEM

If an American citizen believes that another person has hurt him
(by stealing or lying, for example), he can take this person to court. In
the court, both people have lawyers who help to explain the problem.
The first person, Mr. A, explains the problem (testifies) and shows why
and how he was hurt, that is, he gives evidence. The second person, Mr.
B., has the opportunity, chance, to testify and give evidence that shows
he did not hurt Mr. A. After both people have finished testifying, a
decision is made. This decision is made by a jury, twelve American
citizens, or by the judge. If the decision is that Mr. B is guilty, responsible, the judge passes sentence, he tells what the guilty person must do,
such as go to prison or pay a fine, money.

If one of the people is dissatisfied with the process, he can explain
his case to a higher court. The higher court may uphold (keep) or reverse (change) the first court's decision.

This system is very time-consuming (it takes a long time). Sometimes people must wait for a year or more before the court has time to
hear their problems.

1. What do the following words mean?
   a. testify
   b. give evidence
   c. opportunity
   d. jury
   e. guilty
   f. pass sentence
   g. fine
   h. uphold
   i. reverse
   j. time-consuming
2. What do the following refer to?
   a. this person (paragraph 1 line 2)
   b. he (paragraph 1 line 5)
   c. he (paragraph 1 line 7)
   d. he (paragraph 1 line 10)
   e. This system (paragraph 3 line 1)
3. Circle the examples in this passage.
4. Underline the words with prefixes.
5. Write five true–false questions about this passage.
   a.
   b.
   c.
   d.
   e.

Exercise m

Read this passage and answer the questions.

STATE AND LOCAL GOVERNMENTS

The governments of individual states follow the same system as the federal government. There are three branches: legislative, executive, and judicial. The legislative branch makes and changes laws for a state. It decides the age when an individual can begin to drink alcohol, drive a car, etc. The head of the executive branch is the governor. He is elected by all the people in the state. There is a system of state courts very similar to the federal court system. The legislators and the governor usually work in the capital city of the state.

Each city has its own government. The head of city government is the mayor. He works with a group of people called the City Council. They take care of the problems in a city, such as care of the streets, snow removal, and school budgets.

1. What do the following refer to?
    a. It (paragraph 1 line 4)
    b. He (paragraph 1 line 5)
    c. its (paragraph 2 line 1)
    d. He (paragraph 2 line 2)
    e. They (paragraph 2 line 3)
2. Circle all the examples in the passage.
3. Complete the following analogies with the information from the passage.

    a. federal : President :: state : _____

    b. federal : Washington D.C. :: state : _____

    c. state : governor :: city : _____

    d. state : legislature :: city : _____
4. Which government takes care of the following problems? Write the letter of the correct government in the space provided. Guess.
    a. federal
    b. state
    c. city

    _____ Who decides about the budget, money, for a state university?

    _____ Who takes care of the highways in a state?

    _____ Who takes care of the streets in a city?

    _____ Who takes care of the highways between states?